THE ALTERNATIVE MINIMUM TAX

What You Need to Know about the "Other" Income Tax

Harold S. Peckron
Attorney at Law

SPHINX® PUBLISHING
AN IMPRINT OF SOURCEBOOKS, INC.®
NAPERVILLE, ILLINOIS
www.SphinxLegal.com

First Edition, 2005

Published by: **Sphinx® Publishing, An Imprint of Sourcebooks, Inc.®**

Naperville Office
P.O. Box 4410
Naperville, Illinois 60567-4410
630-961-3900
Fax: 630-961-2168
www.sourcebooks.com
www.SphinxLegal.com/Sphinx

Library of Congress Cataloging-in-Publication Data

Peckron, Harold S.
The alternative minimum tax : what you need to know about the "other" income tax / by Harold S. Peckron.-- 1st ed.
p. cm.
Includes bibliographical references and index.
ISBN 1-57248-460-8 (pbk. : alk. paper)
1. Alternative minimum tax--United States--Accounting. 2. Income tax--United States. 3. Tax planning--United States. I. Title.
HJ4653.A7P43 2005
336.24'2--dc22

2005025676

Printed and bound in the United States of America.

BG — 10 9 8 7 6 5 4 3 2 1

Contents

Preface . . . . **vii**

Introduction . . . . **ix**

Chapter 1: Basics of the AMT **1**

Filing Form 6251,
the Alternative Minimum Tax—Individuals

AMT Roadmap

AMT Exemptions

AMT Rates

Capital Gains

Chapter 2: Common AMT Adjustments **21**

Incentive Stock Options

Limitation on Deductions

Chapter 3: Unlikely AMT Adjustments **47**

Alcohol Fuel Credit

Basis Adjustment

Circulation Costs
Depreciation
Installment Sales
Long-Term Contracts
Mining Costs
Net Operating Loss
Passive Activity Losses
Pollution Control Facilities
Tax Shelter Farm Activity

Chapter 4: Tax Preference Items 63

Accelerated Depreciation (pre-1987)
Depletion
Intangible Drilling Costs
Small Business Stock Exclusion
Tax-Exempt Interest

Chapter 5: Importance of the AMT Credits. 79

Nonrefundable Personal Credits
Foreign Tax Credit
Minimum Tax Credit

Chapter 6: AMT Planning 95

Tax Planning
AMT Planning Specifics
Specific AMT Planning Tips
Comprehensive AMT Problems
Final Thoughts

Glossary 143

Appendix A: Alternative Minimum Tax—
Instructions and Form. 153

Appendix B: AMT Audits. 165

Index 187

About the Author. 192

Preface

This book deals with one of the more challenging areas in the tax law—the *alternative minimum tax (AMT)*. Since its origin in the *Tax Reform Act of 1969*, it has steadily affected more and more individual taxpayers—making it a challenge worth understanding. After all, imagine the surprise of a married couple expecting a large refund, only to receive a letter from the IRS demanding a payment of several thousand dollars because of this *stealth tax* known as the AMT. In view of the expanded impact of the AMT on individual taxpayers, it has become essential not only to understand the fundamentals of it, but also to determine the means of planning around it.

The purpose of this book is to lay out, in as much simple English as possible, the basics of the AMT. Will you be capable of filing your own Form 6251, *Alternative Minimum Tax—Individuals*? Perhaps. However, one thing is definite. You will understand why your tax preparer is doing (or not doing) an AMT for you and your family. And even more important, it will give you ways to reduce, or in some cases eliminate, this added tax burden.

The book begins with a brief introduction on the nature of the AMT and computing the AMT (with actual examples and IRS materials). Special chapters on *adjustments* and *tax preference items*, use of the *tax credits* and the importance of the AMT credit, and the oft-overlooked other areas impacting the AMT (like the *kiddie tax* and *estimated tax payments*) follow. The final chapter describes the means to reduce or eliminate the AMT. The chapters have been kept intentionally short and descriptions terse and to the point.

The most beneficial way to master this subject is to read this book from cover to cover. However, you can go straight to the areas or chapters that hold the greatest interest for you.

More importantly, this book is a companion that beats any tax preparer or CPA, because it's on-call 24/7 and aids you in your quest for an answer. If the exact answer is not found, chances are that you will find it at one of the many 24/7 websites identified throughout the book.

As Einstein once said, "The hardest thing in the world to understand is the income tax." This book would have made a believer even out of the late Einstein that taxes need not be complex to gain a basic understanding. Good reading.

Readers with questions can write to the author in care of the publisher:

Sphinx Publishing
P.O. Box 4410
Naperville, IL 60567

—Harold S. Peckron

Introduction

Think of the AMT as a stealth bomber. It will come in virtually undetected, drop its payload on your tax refund, and before you know it, wreak financial devastation. So are you on its trajectory?

Here are a couple of distressing points to keep in mind.

* By 2005, 13 million more taxpayers will pay the AMT, including:
    * 25% earning between $75,000 and $100,000;
    * 46% earning between $100,000 and $200,000; and,
    * 79% earning between $200,000 and $500,000.
* By 2010, 33 million taxpayers—about one-third of all individual taxpayers—will be paying the AMT. In 2013, this figure jumps to 41 million taxpayers.
* The Tax Policy Center predicts that by 2010, taxpayers with incomes *less* than $100,000 will make up 51% of all AMT payers, and practically *all* couples with two children and incomes between $75,000 and $100,000 will be hit with the AMT. In

that same year, about 4 out of 10 taxpayers earning between $50,000 and $75,000 will experience the AMT.

* By 2010, the AMT will account for over $124 billion in government tax revenue or over 9% of the total federal income tax revenue.

The AMT is no longer a tax on the wealthy. With a growing national deficit brought on by increased medical and Social Security costs due to the baby boomers, and with increased military spending to combat terrorism, Congress is *not* about to reduce such a large portion of the federal revenue.

Note: *According to the Wall Street Journal, about 3.3 million taxpayers will pay more in taxes in 2004 because of the AMT. In 2005 (assuming Congress fails to act), that number will increase to 12.3 million.*

In actuality, the AMT is quite basic as a concept. It was designed to force high income individuals and corporations, who continue to pay no regular tax, into making some sort of tax payment. What began as a seemingly viable idea has, over time, become a tragic development in tax law and policy.

To understand how complex the AMT computation is for the average taxpayer, you only need to consider the statement of a former IRS Commissioner who said, *taxpayers should be discouraged from attempting to compute the tax themselves—even with the latest computer software.* But this book will give you the knowledge to ask the right questions, review your current situation with an eye toward reducing the AMT, and perhaps, with a knowledgeable tax preparer, come to more fully understand the AMT.

The AMT dumps numerous tax deductions allowed under the regular tax. Things like the standard deduction, real property taxes, state and city income taxes, exemptions for children, and interest on home equity loans are not allowable deductions in computing your AMT. This makes the tax base—that part you use to compute your tax—a lot larger. In effect, more monies for the IRS.

So how do you know that your particular AMT net is getting larger? Well, you have to compute your tax twice. Once the *old-fashioned way* on your Form 1040 and once again the *AMT way* on the new Form 6251.

While the rest of the world recognizes the ravages of inflation, including the regular tax since 1985 (the regular tax was indexed for inflation in that year), no such luck with the AMT. This means that a middle-class family, in which mom and dad work as two, blue-collar taxpayers with six children and no itemized deductions, will, for purposes of the AMT:

* lose their standard deduction;
* lose their individual personal and six children dependency exemptions; and,
* thanks to cost of living adjustments, have their salaries pushed beyond the AMT exemption amount.

By now you have probably figured out that so long as your AMT is *less* than your regular tax on Form 1040, it will not be a problem. In other words, you pay the greater tax.

2001 and 2003 Tax Acts

The 2001 and 2003 tax acts lowered most American's regular income tax. It did this in a variety of ways—increasing tax deductions and credits, and reducing the basic tax brackets and rates. Unfortunately, the AMT exemption amounts are set to *decrease* in 2005 for all individual taxpayers, while the regular tax rates further decrease. In short, about 13 million more taxpayers will be introduced to the stealth tax for the first time. You may be asking, "Why did the new tax laws not also reduce the AMT?" (How do you think the regular tax reductions were paid for in the first place?)

So while the AMT rates of 26% and 28% may be lower than the top regular tax rate of 35%, the loss of deductions, personal and dependent exemptions, and the lowering of the AMT exemption amount all work together to surprise most taxpayers with a larger tax bill. This means if your AMT is $10,000 and your regular tax is $5,000, you pay the $5,000 in regular tax and the additional AMT tax of $5,000 for a *total tax liability* of $10,000.

AMT Concerns for the Typical Wage Earner

Middle-class wage earners will be experiencing great risk for the AMT. The 2003 tax act made special reductions in the tax rates for dividends and capital gains. These are items of income that most middle-class taxpayers simply do not have or, if they do, the amounts are dwarfed by their salary income. As a result, those who derive their income mainly from investments, as opposed to a salary from a job, will see their taxes decreased at a larger percentage than those who see the majority of their income listed on a W-2.

There are other concerns for the typical wage earner. While the AMT is about 10% below the regular tax rates, many of the most common deductions and exemptions are not allowed in computing the AMT. Even the AMT exemption is phased out as income rises and will be further reduced in 2006. So not only do you get to take fewer deductions, the value of those you do get are lost as your income rises—just when you need them the most. It is for these reasons that the middle-class wage earner will be experiencing great risk for the AMT.

• • • • • •

At this point, you may be feeling less than optimistic. But there is some good news.

There are ways to improve your chances of not being caught in the stealth's trajectory. An entire chapter focuses on these, but one thing is crucial. You must understand the basics and take the appropriate offensive strategy. If you are not proactive, you merely hand over to the government the additional monies because of the AMT. It is up to you to know the rules and use them to your legal advantage to pay less tax.

Case Study:

Mr. and Mrs. Jones live in the beautiful, albeit high tax state of California. They both work, earning over $250,000 with about $25,000 in California property taxes and income taxes. They have two children ready for college in 2003. A life-long friend of the family, Mr. Smith, who owns a financial planning and investment firm, counseled the Jones to borrow against their home's equity for the children's shortfall in college funds.

Without investigating the possible tax consequences, the Jones did as advised. In 2002, their regular tax liabilty amounted to slightly over $50,000, with no AMT problem. They had taken, among other deductions, their state, local, and property taxes, and their exemptions.

In 2003, the real property and state income taxes increased because their salaries had increased with inflation, plus they had the interest deduction from the $100,000 home equity loan. For 2003, their regular (Form 1040) tax liability was even less than their 2002 regular tax liability, or about $50,000. However, the AMT (Form 6251) tax liability was almost $10,000 more, or close to $60,000. Why? You probably figured it out. No deductions for the home equity interest, property taxes, state income taxes, and no exemptions.

The moral?

Understand the AMT consequences before you pursue a given financial strategy.

Advisors in any field are not infallible. Plus, in most cases, they cannot be held accountable if they are using their best judgment and it is simply wrong. You, on the other hand, should recognize the importance of understanding the consequences of the selected option.

Publisher's Note: *The final version of some of the forms found throughout this text may not have been available at the time this book went to press. If the final version was not available, the Internal Revenue Service's official draft version was used in its place. Check with the IRS at 800-TAX-FORM or go to* ***www.irs.gov*** *for the latest version of any form.*

chapter one:

Basics of the AMT

Imagine that you have completed your tax return for the year and expect a large refund. Some months later, you receive a notice from the IRS that not only eliminates the refund, but also demands an additional sum because of something known as the *alternative minimum tax* (AMT). Not knowing what this *alternative* tax means, you ponder whether this is an error.

Welcome to the new world of federal income tax that will begin to affect millions of Americans.

Originating in the 1960's, the alternative minimum tax for individuals was designed to ensure that high-income individuals would pay *some minimum amount* of tax. That was then. Now the AMT is set to cause financial havoc for most middle-class taxpayers. It is a second, parallel tax, in which taxpayers are hit with a loss of deductions resulting in higher taxes. Think of it, however, as a true additional tax—you must pay the regular tax and, if the AMT is greater, the *excess* is then added to the regular tax. Result: an increased tax bill.

Because of complexity and tax differences, the AMT poses many challenges to the average taxpayer. In other words, certain deductions that are allowed for the so-called *regular tax* (what most taxpayers compute on Form 1040) are denied for the AMT. (More differences between the two tax systems will become apparent as your reading continues.)

On my office wall I have the original tax form that individuals used in the first year of filing their federal taxes in 1913. It is one page in length—including the instructions! Fast forward to 2004. Go to the IRS website—**www.irs.gov**—and click on the "Forms and Publications" link. The sheer number of forms will amaze you. And, of course, every time Congress tinkers with the tax law, the relevant forms need to be revised.

Section 2004 of the IRS *Restructuring and Reform Act of 1998* requires the U.S. Treasury to develop procedures for a return-free tax system for certain individual taxpayers no later than 2007. Does this mean that you will not be filing a tax return for the regular tax (Form 1040) or the AMT (Form 6251)? Not according to the December 2003 U.S. Treasury Report to Congress. Only about 52 million taxpayers (those primarily with all withholding income) will be exempt from filing. So most individual taxpayers will still need to file using the IRS forms.

Form **1040** Department of the Treasury—Internal Revenue Service
U.S. Individual Income Tax Return 2004 (99) IRS Use Only—Do not write or staple in this space.

For the year Jan. 1–Dec. 31, 2004, or other tax year beginning , 2004, ending , 20 | OMB No. 1545-0074

Label (See instructions on page 19.)
Use the IRS label. Otherwise, please print or type.

LABEL HERE

Your first name and initial	Last name		**Your social security number**
If a joint return, spouse's first name and initial	Last name		**Spouse's social security number**
Home address (number and street). If you have a P.O. box, see page 19.		Apt. no.	▲ **Important!** ▲ You **must** enter your SSN(s) above.
City, town or post office, state, and ZIP code. If you have a foreign address, see page 19.			

Presidential Election Campaign (See page 19.)
Note. Checking "Yes" will not change your tax or reduce your refund.
Do you, or your spouse if filing a joint return, want $3 to go to this fund? ▶ **You** ☐ **Yes** ☐ **No** **Spouse** ☐ **Yes** ☐ **No**

Filing Status
Check only one box.

1 ☐ Single
2 ☐ Married filing jointly (even if only one had income)
3 ☐ Married filing separately. Enter spouse's SSN above and full name here. ▶
4 ☐ Head of household (with qualifying person). (See page 20.) If the qualifying person is a child but not your dependent, enter this child's name here. ▶
5 ☐ Qualifying widow(er) with dependent child (see page 20)

Exemptions

6a ☐ **Yourself.** If someone can claim you as a dependent, **do not** check box 6a
b ☐ **Spouse**
c **Dependents:**

(1) First name Last name	(2) Dependent's social security number	(3) Dependent's relationship to you	(4) ✓ if qualifying child for child tax credit (see page 21)
			☐
			☐
			☐
			☐

If more than four dependents, see page 21.

d Total number of exemptions claimed

Boxes checked on 6a and 6b ____
No. of children on 6c who:
• **lived with you** ____
• **did not live with you due to divorce or separation (see page 21)** ____
Dependents on 6c not entered above ____
Add numbers on lines above ▶ ☐

Income

Attach Forms W-2 here. Also attach Form(s) W-2G and 1099-R if tax was withheld.

If you did not get a W-2, see page 22.

Enclose, but do not attach, any payment. Also, please use **Form 1040-V.**

7	Wages, salaries, tips, etc. Attach Form(s) W-2	7	
8a	**Taxable** interest. Attach Schedule B if required	8a	
b	**Tax-exempt** interest. **Do not** include on line 8a — 8b		
9a	Ordinary dividends. Attach Schedule B if required	9a	
b	Qualified dividends (see page 23) — 9b		
10	Taxable refunds, credits, or offsets of state and local income taxes (see page 23)	10	
11	Alimony received	11	
12	Business income or (loss). Attach Schedule C or C-EZ	12	
13	Capital gain or (loss). Attach Schedule D if required. If not required, check here ▶ ☐	13	
14	Other gains or (losses). Attach Form 4797	14	
15a	IRA distributions — 15a — b Taxable amount (see page 25)	15b	
16a	Pensions and annuities — 16a — b Taxable amount (see page 25)	16b	
17	Rental real estate, royalties, partnerships, S corporations, trusts, etc. Attach Schedule E	17	
18	Farm income or (loss). Attach Schedule F	18	
19	Unemployment compensation	19	
20a	Social security benefits — 20a — b Taxable amount (see page 27)	20b	
21	Other income. List type and amount (see page 27)	21	
22	Add the amounts in the far right column for lines 7 through 21. This is your **total income** ▶	22	

Adjusted Gross Income

23	Deduction for clean-fuel vehicles (see page 29)	23	
24	Certain business expenses of reservists, performing artists, and fee-basis government officials. Attach Form 2106 or 2106-EZ	24	
25	IRA deduction (see page 29)	25	
26	Student loan interest deduction (see page 31)	26	
27	Tuition and fees deduction (see page 32)	27	
28	Health savings account deduction. Attach Form 8889	28	
29	Moving expenses. Attach Form 3903	29	
30	One-half of self-employment tax. Attach Schedule SE	30	
31	Self-employed health insurance deduction (see page 33)	31	
32	Self-employed SEP, SIMPLE, and qualified plans	32	
33	Penalty on early withdrawal of savings	33	
34a	Alimony paid **b** Recipient's SSN ▶	34a	
35	Add lines 23 through 34a	35	
36	Subtract line 35 from line 22. This is your **adjusted gross income** ▶	36	

For Disclosure, Privacy Act, and Paperwork Reduction Act Notice, see page 77. Cat. No. 11320B Form **1040** (2004)

Form 1040 (2004) Page 2

Tax and Credits

Standard Deduction for—
- People who checked any box on line 38a or 38b or who can be claimed as a dependent, see page 34.
- All others:

Single or Married filing separately, $4,850

Married filing jointly or Qualifying widow(er), $9,700

Head of household, $7,150

37	Amount from line 36 (adjusted gross income)		37
38a	Check if: ☐ **You** were born before January 2, 1940, ☐ Blind. ☐ **Spouse** was born before January 2, 1940, ☐ Blind. **Total boxes checked** ▶ 38a		
b	If you are married filing separately and your spouse itemizes deductions, or you were a dual-status alien, see page 34 and check here ▶ 38b ☐		
39	**Itemized deductions** (from Schedule A) **or** your **standard deduction** (see left margin)		39
40	Subtract line 39 from line 37		40
41	If line 37 is $107,025 or less, multiply $3,100 by the total number of exemptions claimed on line 6d. If line 37 is over $107,025, see the worksheet on page 35		41
42	**Taxable income.** Subtract line 41 from line 40. If line 41 is more than line 40, enter -0-		42
43	**Tax** (see page 36). Check if any tax is from: **a** ☐ Form(s) 8814 **b** ☐ Form 4972		43
44	**Alternative minimum tax** (see page 38). Attach Form 6251		44
45	Add lines 43 and 44 ▶		45
46	Credit for child and dependent care expenses. Attach Form 2441	46	
47	Credit for the elderly or the disabled. Attach Schedule R	47	
48	Education credits. Attach Form 8863	48	
49	Credits from: **a** ☐ Form 8396 **b** ☐ Form 8859	49	
50	Foreign tax credit. Attach Form 1116 if required	50	
51	Child tax credit (see page 40)	51	
52	Retirement savings contributions credit. Attach Form 8880	52	
53	Adoption credit. Attach Form 8839	53	
54	Other credits. Check applicable box(es): **a** ☐ Form 3800 **b** ☐ Form 8801 **c** ☐ Specify ______	54	
55	Add lines 46 through 54. These are your **total credits**		55
56	Subtract line 55 from line 45. If line 55 is more than line 45, enter -0- ▶		56

Other Taxes

57	Self-employment tax. Attach Schedule SE	57
58	Social security and Medicare tax on tip income not reported to employer. Attach Form 4137	58
59	Additional tax on IRAs, other qualified retirement plans, etc. Attach Form 5329 if required	59
60	Advance earned income credit payments from Form(s) W-2	60
61	Household employment taxes. Attach Schedule H	61
62	Add lines 56 through 61. This is your **total tax** ▶	62

Payments

If you have a qualifying child, attach Schedule EIC.

63	Federal income tax withheld from Forms W-2 and 1099	63	
64	2004 estimated tax payments and amount applied from 2003 return	64	
65	**Earned income credit (EIC)**	65	
66	Excess social security and tier 1 RRTA tax withheld (see page 56)	66	
67	Additional child tax credit. Attach Form 8812	67	
68	Amount paid with request for extension to file (see page 56)	68	
69	Other payments from: **a** ☐ Form 2439 **b** ☐ Form 4136 **c** ☐ Form 8885	69	
70	Add lines 63 through 69. These are your **total payments** ▶		70

Refund

Direct deposit? See page 56 and fill in 72b, 72c, and 72d.

71	If line 70 is more than line 62, subtract line 62 from line 70. This is the amount you **overpaid**		71
72a	Amount of line 71 you want **refunded to you** ▶		72a
▶ b	Routing number ☐☐☐☐☐☐☐☐☐ ▶ **c** Type: ☐ Checking ☐ Savings		
▶ d	Account number ☐☐☐☐☐☐☐☐☐☐☐☐☐☐☐☐☐		
73	Amount of line 71 you want **applied to your 2005 estimated tax** ▶	73	

Amount You Owe

74	**Amount you owe.** Subtract line 70 from line 62. For details on how to pay, see page 57 ▶		74
75	Estimated tax penalty (see page 58)	75	

Third Party Designee

Do you want to allow another person to discuss this return with the IRS (see page 58)? ☐ **Yes.** Complete the following. ☐ **No**

Designee's name ▶ Phone no. ▶ ( ) Personal identification number (PIN) ▶ ☐☐☐☐☐

Sign Here

Joint return? See page 20.

Keep a copy for your records.

Under penalties of perjury, I declare that I have examined this return and accompanying schedules and statements, and to the best of my knowledge and belief, they are true, correct, and complete. Declaration of preparer (other than taxpayer) is based on all information of which preparer has any knowledge.

Your signature	Date	Your occupation	Daytime phone number ( )
Spouse's signature. If a joint return, **both** must sign.	Date	Spouse's occupation	

Paid Preparer's Use Only

Preparer's signature ▶	Date	Check if self-employed ☐	Preparer's SSN or PTIN
Firm's name (or yours if self-employed), address, and ZIP code ▶		EIN	
		Phone no. ( )	

Form **1040** (2004)

Printed on recycled paper

Filing Form 6251, the Alternative Minimum Tax—Individuals

First, you must decide whether or not you must file the AMT form. In simple terms—ask yourself whether the taxable income on Form 1040, combined with certain AMT adjustments (discussed in Chapters 2 and 3) and AMT tax preference items (discussed in Chapter 4), exceeds the AMT exemptions.

Note: *In 2006, unless Congress changes it, the AMT exemptions of $58,000, $40,250, and $29,000 will revert to their lower respective amounts of $45,000, $33,750, and $22,500.*

Example 1:

Maria, a single taxpayer, has a taxable income on her Form 1040 of $75,000, and combined AMT adjustments and preferences of $20,000, for a total of $95,000. Since this exceeds her AMT exemption of $40,250, she must file Form 6251.

AMT Exemptions 2003–2004

$58,000—Married Filing Jointly and Surviving Spouse

$40,250—Single or Head of Household

$29,000—Married Filing a Separate Return

Example 2:

Eldon, a married taxpayer and sole breadwinner, has a taxable income of $40,000, with AMT adjustments and preferences of $10,000, for a sum of $50,000. He will not need to file Form 6251 because his exemption of $58,000 exceeds this amount.

In close calculations, such as Eldon's from the previous example, you should use the worksheet provided in the Form 1040 instructions. After completing your regular income tax return, use the worksheet to determine whether your tax deductions and credits may have reduced your taxes below the AMT threshold. (This can save completing the 55-line Form 6251.) A copy of the 2003 worksheet is on the following page.

Line 42

Alternative Minimum Tax

Use the worksheet below to see if you should fill in **Form 6251.**

Exception. Fill in Form 6251 instead of using the worksheet below if you claimed or received **any** of the following items.

- Accelerated depreciation.
- Stock by exercising an incentive stock option and you did not dispose of the stock in the same year.
- Tax-exempt interest from private activity bonds.
- Intangible drilling, circulation, research, experimental, or mining costs.
- Amortization of pollution-control facilities or depletion.
- Income or (loss) from tax-shelter farm activities or passive activities.
- Income from long-term contracts not figured using the percentage-of-completion method.
- Interest paid on a home mortgage **not** used to buy, build, or substantially improve your home.
- Investment interest expense reported on **Form 4952.**
- Net operating loss deduction.
- Alternative minimum tax adjustments from an estate, trust, electing large partnership, or cooperative.
- Section 1202 exclusion.

Worksheet To See if You Should Fill in Form 6251—Line 42

Keep for Your Records

Before you begin:

√ Be sure you have read the **Exception** above to see if you must fill in Form 6251 instead of using this worksheet.

√ If you are claiming the foreign tax credit (see the instructions for Form 1040, line 44, on page 39), enter that credit on line 44.

1. Are you filing **Schedule A?**
☐ **Yes.** Enter the amount from Form 1040, line 38.
☐ **No.** Enter the amount from Form 1040, line 35, and go to line 4 .... **1.** ______

2. Enter the **smaller** of the amount on Schedule A, line 4, or 2.5% (.025) of the amount on Form 1040, line 35 .... **2.** ______

3. Enter the total of the amounts from Schedule A, lines 9 and 26 .... **3.** ______

4. Add lines 1 through 3 above .... **4.** ______

5. Enter the amount shown below for your filing status.
- Single or head of household—$40,250
- Married filing jointly or qualifying widow(er)—$58,000
- Married filing separately—$29,000 .... **5.** ______

6. Is the amount on line 4 more than the amount on line 5?
☐ **No.** STOP You do not need to fill in Form 6251.
☐ **Yes.** Subtract line 5 from line 4 .... **6.** ______

7. Enter the amount shown below for your filing status.
- Single or head of household—$112,500
- Married filing jointly or qualifying widow(er)—$150,000
- Married filing separately—$75,000 .... **7.** ______

8. Is the amount on line 4 more than the amount on line 7?
☐ **No.** Enter the amount from line 6 on line 10 and go to line 11.
☐ **Yes.** Subtract line 7 from line 4 .... **8.** ______

9. Multiply line 8 by 25% (.25) and enter the result but do not enter more than line 5 above .... **9.** ______

10. Add lines 6 and 9 .... **10.** ______

11. Is the amount on line 10 more than $175,000 ($87,500 if married filing separately)?
☐ **Yes.** STOP Fill in Form 6251 to see if you owe the alternative minimum tax.
☐ **No.** Multiply line 10 by 26% (.26) .... **11.** ______

12. Enter the amount from Form 1040, line 41, minus the total of any tax from Form 4972 and any amount on Form 1040, line 44 .... **12.** ______

Next. Is the amount on line 11 more than the amount on line 12?
☐ **Yes.** Fill in Form 6251 to see if you owe the alternative minimum tax.
☐ **No.** You do not need to fill in Form 6251.

AMT Roadmap

A roadmap or diagram of the basic structure of the AMT and the process of calculating your tax liability may help.

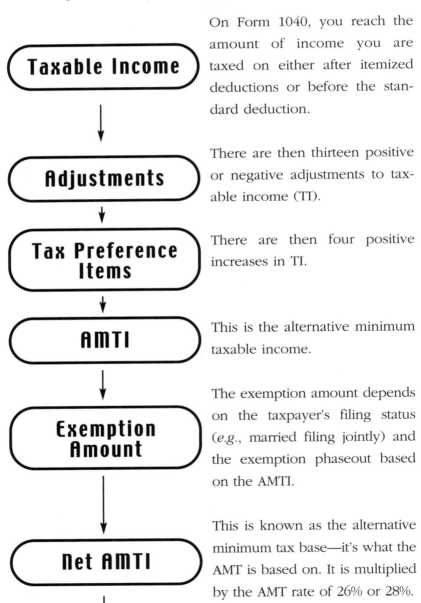

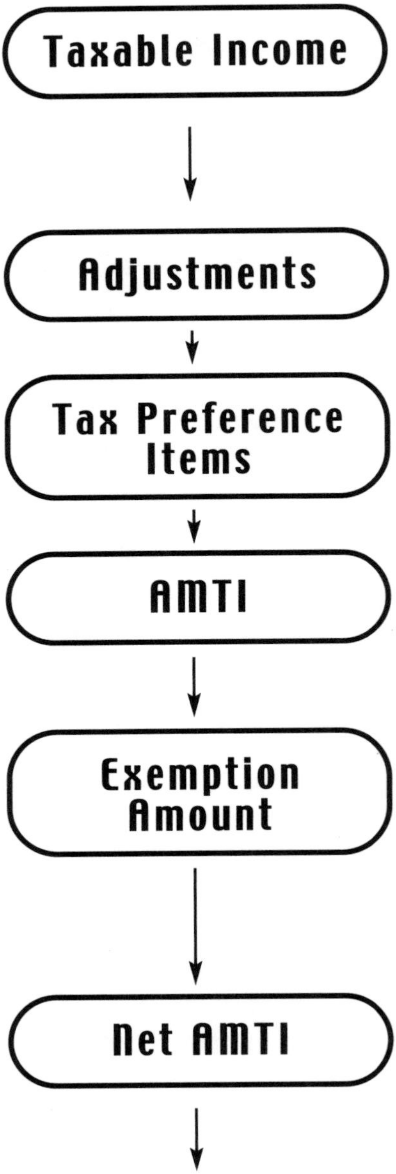

On Form 1040, you reach the amount of income you are taxed on either after itemized deductions or before the standard deduction.

There are then thirteen positive or negative adjustments to taxable income (TI).

There are then four positive increases in TI.

This is the alternative minimum taxable income.

The exemption amount depends on the taxpayer's filing status (*e.g.*, married filing jointly) and the exemption phaseout based on the AMTI.

This is known as the alternative minimum tax base—it's what the AMT is based on. It is multiplied by the AMT rate of 26% or 28%.

AMT

Notice that this AMT amount may not be the actual AMT paid.

↓

AMTFTC

For taxpayers with any foreign taxes paid, the AMTFTC reduces the AMTI dollar for dollar.

↓

Tentative AMT

This is the tentative AMT liability, but is still not necessarily the final AMT.

↓

Regular Tax

Line 43 on the 2004 Form 1040.

↓

Is AMT Greater than Regular Tax?

↓ **Yes** ↓

Pay the AMT on Form 6251 (this is actually two components—the regular tax and the AMT)

↓ **No** ↓

Pay the regular tax on Form 1040

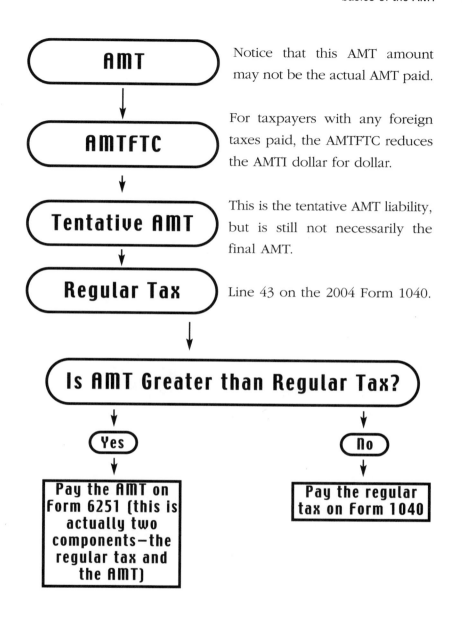

Exemption Worksheet—Line 29

Keep for Your Records

Note: *If Form 6251, line 28, is equal to or more than: $273,500 if single or head of household; $382,000 if married filing jointly or qualifying widow(er); or $191,000 if married filing separately; your exemption is zero.* ***Do not*** *complete this worksheet; instead, enter the amount from Form 6251, line 28, on line 30 and go to line 31.*

1. Enter: $40,250 if single or head of household; $58,000 if married filing jointly or qualifying widow(er); $29,000 if married filing separately . . . . **1.** ______

2. Enter your alternative minimum taxable income (AMTI) from Form 6251, line 28 . . . **2.** ______

3. Enter: $112,500 if single or head of household; $150,000 if married filing jointly or qualifying widow(er); $75,000 if married filing separately . . . . . . **3.** ______

4. Subtract line 3 from line 2. If zero or less, enter -0- . . . . . . **4.** ______

5. Multiply line 4 by 25% (.25) . . . . **5.** ______

6. Subtract line 5 from line 1. If zero or less, enter -0-. If this form is for a child under age 14, go to line 7 below. Otherwise, **stop here** and enter this amount on Form 6251, line 29, and go to Form 6251, line 30 . . . . . . ▶ **6.** ______

7. Child's minimum exemption amount **7.** $5,600

8. Enter the **child's earned income,** if any (see instructions) . . . . **8.** ______

9. Add lines 7 and 8 . . . . **9.** ______

10. Enter the **smaller** of line 6 or line 9 here and on Form 6251, line 29, and go to Form 6251, line 30 . . . . . . ▶ **10.** ______

AMT Exemptions

The AMT *exemption* is zero if the *alternative minimum taxable income* (AMTI) reaches:

$382,000, and you are married filing jointly or surviving spouse;

$273,500, and you are single; or,

$191,000, and you are married filing separately.

As the roadmap on page 8 indicates, a key calculation is the exemption amount. An *exemption amount* means that the taxpayer may have no AMT liability. To further assist a taxpayer in deciding whether it may be necessary to complete Form 6251, the IRS provides an AMT exemption worksheet. The worksheet attempts to simplify the reduction calculations of the exemption amount.

The AMT exemptions are phased out once your income reaches a certain level. In 2003 through 2005, the exemption amounts of $58,000, $40,250, and $29,000 are reduced by a formula once your AMT taxable income exceeds:

- $150,000 for married filing jointly and surviving spouses;
- $112,500 for single individuals; and,
- $75,000 for married filing separately.

In certain cases, your AMT exemption amount is completely phased out in 2003, 2004, and 2005 whenever the following occurs.

The AMT exemption phaseout for married filing separately is equal to the phaseout for married filing jointly taxpayers ($191,000 x 2 = $382,000). However, if the married filing separately taxpayer's AMTI exceeds $191,000, then a special *add back* computation is required. Such a calculation demands that the AMTI be increased by 25% of the amount over \$191,000, limited to the AMT exemption amount of \$29,000. So the full \$29,000 *add back* makes the AMTI limit for married filing separately \$307,000.

Example:

In 2004, Bart and his spouse file married filing jointly and compute their AMTI to be \$175,000. This reduces their AMT exemption of \$58,000 in that year to \$51,750, as follows:

$$\$58,000 - .25(\$175,000 - \$150,000) = \$51,750$$

Had the couple's AMTI been \$382,000, no AMT exemption would be allowed:

$$\$58,000 - .25(\$382,000 - \$150,000) = \$0$$

Note: *Special rules exist for the AMT exemption available to minor children (under age 14) and are set forth in the Instructions to Form 6251.*

It is important that you realize this computation must be performed *every* year. The fact that you are or are not subject to the AMT in one year has no bearing on whether you are liable for the AMT in a succeeding year. Every year stands on its own.

The AMT is actually comprised of *two* taxes. Your total tax due is comprised of the AMT *and* your regular tax.

(This makes the taxpayer's AMT burden that of an additional tax beyond the regular tax.)

Example:

Donald and Sue file married filing jointly in 2003. Their regular tax (Form 1040) liability amounts to $18,851.98 and their AMT (Form 6251) liability is $14,864. In 2003 they are liable for a regular tax of $18,851.98, because they pay the larger of the two taxes.

In 2004, their regular tax liability is $25,291.52, but their AMT liability results in $32,555.45. Here, unlike 2003, they owe an AMT liability of $32,555.45 (because it is the larger of the two), comprised of $25,291.52 of regular tax and $7,263.93 of AMT.

(Even though the IRS considers these to be two taxes, you can generally just assume that your tax liability is the greater of the two taxes and need not think of them as two taxes.)

AMT Rates

Another characteristic of the AMT that causes it to affect more and more people every year is that the income brackets tied to its rates are not indexed for inflation. So, for example, if cost of living goes up 3% from one year to the next, the AMT income bracket stays fixed, causing you to have more of your income affected by the AMT rates. The regular tax is indexed for inflation, so generally speaking, every year the size of the income brackets increases for each tax rate percentage.

The actual AMT tax rate is 26% on the first $175,000 of AMTI. Any excess AMTI is taxed at a flat 28%. So, unlike the progressive nature of the regular tax, which has rates ranging from 10% to 35% and is calculated with tax tables and schedules, the AMT has only two tax rates. All AMTI is either equal to or less than $175,000 *or* is over $175,000.

Flat Tax Rate

For married filing jointly and surviving spouse, or single:

Over	But Not Over	Pay+	% on Excess	Of the Amount Over
$0	$175,000	$0+	26%	$0
$175,000	—	$45,500+	28%	$175,000

For married filing separately:

Over	But Not Over	Pay+	% on Excess	Of the Amount Over
$0	$87,500	$0+	26%	$0
$87,500	—	$32,750+	28%	$87,500

Example:

Ron, a single individual, has an AMTI of $300,000. His AMT liability (before credits) is $80,500.

(.26 x $175,000) + (.28 x $125,000) = $80,500

Form **6251**

Department of the Treasury
Internal Revenue Service (99)

Alternative Minimum Tax—Individuals

▶ See separate instructions.

▶ Attach to Form 1040 or Form 1040NR.

OMB No. 1545-0227

2004

Attachment Sequence No. 32

Name(s) shown on Form 1040 | Your social security number

Part I **Alternative Minimum Taxable Income** (See instructions for how to complete each line.)

1	If filing Schedule A (Form 1040), enter the amount from Form 1040, line 40, and go to line 2. Otherwise, enter the amount from Form 1040, line 37, and go to line 7. (If zero or less, enter as a negative amount.)	1	
2	Medical and dental. Enter the **smaller** of Schedule A (Form 1040), line 4, **or** 2½% of Form 1040, line 37	2	
3	Taxes from Schedule A (Form 1040), line 9	3	
4	Enter the home mortgage interest adjustment, if any, from line 6 of the worksheet on page 2 of the instructions	4	
5	Miscellaneous deductions from Schedule A (Form 1040), line 26	5	
6	If Form 1040, line 37, is over $142,700 (over $71,350 if married filing separately), enter the amount from line 9 of the **Itemized Deductions Worksheet** on page A-6 of the Schedule A (Form 1040) instructions	6	( )
7	Tax refund from Form 1040, line 10 or line 21	7	( )
8	Investment interest expense (difference between regular tax and AMT)	8	
9	Depletion (difference between regular tax and AMT)	9	
10	Net operating loss deduction from Form 1040, line 21. Enter as a positive amount	10	
11	Interest from specified private activity bonds exempt from the regular tax	11	
12	Qualified small business stock (7% of gain excluded under section 1202)	12	
13	Exercise of incentive stock options (excess of AMT income over regular tax income)	13	
14	Estates and trusts (amount from Schedule K-1 (Form 1041), line 9)	14	
15	Electing large partnerships (amount from Schedule K-1 (Form 1065-B), box 6)	15	
16	Disposition of property (difference between AMT and regular tax gain or loss)	16	
17	Depreciation on assets placed in service after 1986 (difference between regular tax and AMT)	17	
18	Passive activities (difference between AMT and regular tax income or loss)	18	
19	Loss limitations (difference between AMT and regular tax income or loss)	19	
20	Circulation costs (difference between regular tax and AMT)	20	
21	Long-term contracts (difference between AMT and regular tax income)	21	
22	Mining costs (difference between regular tax and AMT)	22	
23	Research and experimental costs (difference between regular tax and AMT)	23	
24	Income from certain installment sales before January 1, 1987	24	( )
25	Intangible drilling costs preference	25	
26	Other adjustments, including income-based related adjustments	26	
27	Alternative tax net operating loss deduction	27	( )
28	**Alternative minimum taxable income.** Combine lines 1 through 27. (If married filing separately and line 28 is more than $191,000, see page 7 of the instructions.)	28	

Part II **Alternative Minimum Tax**

29 Exemption. (If this form is for a child under age 14, see page 7 of the instructions.)

IF your filing status is . . .	AND line 28 is not over . . .	THEN enter on line 29 . . .
Single or head of household	$112,500	$40,250
Married filing jointly or qualifying widow(er)	150,000	58,000
Married filing separately	75,000	29,000

If line 28 is **over** the amount shown above for your filing status, see page 7 of the instructions. — 29

30	Subtract line 29 from line 28. If zero or less, enter -0- here and on lines 33 and 35 and stop here	30	
31	• If you reported capital gain distributions directly on Form 1040, line 13; you reported qualified dividends on Form 1040, line 9b; **or** you had a gain on both lines 15 and 16 of Schedule D (Form 1040) (as refigured for the AMT, if necessary), complete Part III on the back and enter the amount from line 55 here. • **All others:** If line 30 is $175,000 or less ($87,500 or less if married filing separately), multiply line 30 by 26% (.26). Otherwise, multiply line 30 by 28% (.28) and subtract $3,500 ($1,750 if married filing separately) from the result.	31	
32	Alternative minimum tax foreign tax credit (see page 7 of the instructions)	32	
33	Tentative minimum tax. Subtract line 32 from line 31	33	
34	Tax from Form 1040, line 43 (minus any tax from Form 4972 and any foreign tax credit from Form 1040, line 50)	34	
35	**Alternative minimum tax.** Subtract line 34 from line 33. If zero or less, enter -0-. Enter here and on Form 1040, line 44	35	

For Paperwork Reduction Act Notice, see page 8 of the instructions. Cat. No. 13600G Form **6251** (2004)

Form 6251 (2004) Page 2

Part III Tax Computation Using Maximum Capital Gains Rates

36	Enter the amount from Form 6251, line 30		36
37	Enter the amount from line 6 of the Qualified Dividends and Capital Gain Tax Worksheet in the instructions for Form 1040, line 43, or the amount from line 13 of the Schedule D Tax Worksheet on page D-11 of the instructions for Schedule D (Form 1040), whichever applies (as refigured for the AMT, if necessary) (see page 8 of the instructions)	37	
38	Enter the amount from Schedule D (Form 1040), line 19 (as refigured for the AMT, if necessary) (see page 8 of the instructions)	38	
39	If you did not complete a Schedule D Tax Worksheet for the regular tax or the AMT, enter the amount from line 37. Otherwise, add lines 37 and 38, and enter the **smaller** of that result or the amount from line 10 of the Schedule D Tax Worksheet (as refigured for the AMT, if necessary)	39	
40	Enter the **smaller** of line 36 or line 39		40
41	Subtract line 40 from line 36		41
42	If line 41 is $175,000 or less ($87,500 or less if married filing separately), multiply line 41 by 26% (.26). Otherwise, multiply line 41 by 28% (.28) and subtract $3,500 ($1,750 if married filing separately) from the result ▶		42
43	Enter the **smaller** of line 36 or: • $58,100 if married filing jointly or qualifying widow(er), • $29,050 if single or married filing separately, or • $38,900 if head of household.	43	
44	Enter the amount from line 7 of the Qualified Dividends and Capital Gain Tax Worksheet in the instructions for Form 1040, line 43, or the amount from line 14 of the Schedule D Tax Worksheet on page D-11 of the instructions for Schedule D (Form 1040), whichever applies (as figured for the regular tax)	44	
45	Subtract line 44 from line 43. If zero or less, enter -0-	45	
46	Enter the **smaller** of line 36 or line 37	46	
47	Enter the **smaller** of line 45 or line 46	47	
48	Multiply line 47 by 5% (.05) ▶		48
49	Subtract line 47 from line 46	49	
50	Multiply line 49 by 15% (.15) ▶		50
	If line 38 is zero or blank, skip lines 51 and 52 and go to line 53. Otherwise, go to line 51.		
51	Subtract line 46 from line 40	51	
52	Multiply line 51 by 25% (.25) ▶		52
53	Add lines 42, 48, 50, and 52		53
54	If line 36 is $175,000 or less ($87,500 or less if married filing separately), multiply line 36 by 26% (.26). Otherwise, multiply line 36 by 28% (.28) and subtract $3,500 ($1,750 if married filing separately) from the result		54
55	Enter the **smaller** of line 53 or line 54 here and on line 31		55

Printed on recycled paper

Form **6251** (2004)

Capital Gains

When you look at Form 6251, you will notice that it is only a two-page form. But on the second page is a section entitled "Part III: Tax Computation Using Maximum Capital Gains Rates."

When is Part III on page 2 necessary?

Whenever a taxpayer has *long-term capital gains* that require a holding period that exceeds one year *or* capital gains distributions taxed at 15% for regular tax (Form 1040) purposes. Such gains and distributions (as from a mutual fund) are also taxed at those rates in the AMT. You must carve out these capital gains. This is the *purpose* of Part III.

There is an easy way to decide whether a Part III computation may be necessary. If you used Schedule D when completing your Form 1040, review Part III and follow its instructions.

Note: *A large capital gain, despite Part III of Form 6251, may disqualify your AMT exemption. Timing of capital gains is important, as the capital gain income is included in the income phaseout of the AMT exemption.*

SCHEDULE D (Form 1040)

Department of the Treasury Internal Revenue Service (99)

Capital Gains and Losses

▶ Attach to Form 1040. ▶ See Instructions for Schedule D (Form 1040).

▶ Use Schedule D-1 to list additional transactions for lines 1 and 8.

OMB No. 1545-0074

2004

Attachment Sequence No. 12

Name(s) shown on Form 1040

Your social security number

Part I Short-Term Capital Gains and Losses—Assets Held One Year or Less

(a) Description of property (Example: 100 sh. XYZ Co.)	(b) Date acquired (Mo., day, yr.)	(c) Date sold (Mo., day, yr.)	(d) Sales price (see page D-6 of the instructions)	(e) Cost or other basis (see page D-6 of the instructions)	(f) Gain or (loss) Subtract (e) from (d)
1					

2 Enter your short-term totals, if any, from Schedule D-1, line 2	2			
3 **Total short-term sales price amounts.** Add lines 1 and 2 in column (d)	3			
4 Short-term gain from Form 6252 and short-term gain or (loss) from Forms 4684, 6781, and 8824			4	
5 Net short-term gain or (loss) from partnerships, S corporations, estates, and trusts from Schedule(s) K-1			5	
6 Short-term capital loss carryover. Enter the amount, if any, from line 8 of your **Capital Loss Carryover Worksheet** on page D-5 of the Instructions			6	( )
7 **Net short-term capital gain or (loss).** Combine lines 1 through 6 in column (f)			7	

Part II Long-Term Capital Gains and Losses—Assets Held More Than One Year

(a) Description of property (Example: 100 sh. XYZ Co.)	(b) Date acquired (Mo., day, yr.)	(c) Date sold (Mo., day, yr.)	(d) Sales price (see page D-6 of the instructions)	(e) Cost or other basis (see page D-6 of the instructions)	(f) Gain or (loss) Subtract (e) from (d)
8					

9 Enter your long-term totals, if any, from Schedule D-1, line 9	9			
10 **Total long-term sales price amounts.** Add lines 8 and 9 in column (d)	10			
11 Gain from Form 4797, Part I; long-term gain from Forms 2439 and 6252; and long-term gain or (loss) from Forms 4684, 6781, and 8824			11	
12 Net long-term gain or (loss) from partnerships, S corporations, estates, and trusts from Schedule(s) K-1			12	
13 Capital gain distributions. See page D-2 of the instructions			13	
14 Long-term capital loss carryover. Enter the amount, if any, from line 13 of your **Capital Loss Carryover Worksheet** on page D-5 of the Instructions			14	( )
15 **Net long-term capital gain or (loss).** Combine lines 8 through 14 in column (f). Then go to Part III on the back			15	

For Paperwork Reduction Act Notice, see Form 1040 instructions. Cat. No. 11338H **Schedule D (Form 1040) 2004**

Schedule D (Form 1040) 2004 Page **2**

Part III **Summary**

16 Combine lines 7 and 15 and enter the result. If line 16 is a loss, skip lines 17 through 20, and go to line 21. If a gain, enter the gain on Form 1040, line 13	**16**		
17 Are lines 15 and 16 **both** gains? ☐ **Yes.** Go to line 18. ☐ **No.** Skip lines 18 through 21, and go to line 22.			
18 Enter the amount, if any, from line 7 of the **28% Rate Gain Worksheet** on page D-7 of the instructions . . . . ▶	**18**		
19 Enter the amount, if any, from line 18 of the **Unrecaptured Section 1250 Gain Worksheet** on page D-8 of the instructions . . . . ▶	**19**		
20 Are lines 18 and 19 **both** zero or blank? ☐ **Yes.** Complete Form 1040 through line 42, and then complete the **Qualified Dividends and Capital Gain Tax Worksheet** on page 37 of the Instructions for Form 1040. **Do not** complete lines 21 and 22 below. ☐ **No.** Complete the **Schedule D Tax Worksheet** on page D-10 of the instructions. **Do not** complete lines 21 and 22 below.			
21 If line 16 is a loss, enter here and on Form 1040, line 13, the **smaller** of: • The loss on line 16 or • ($3,000), or if married filing separately, ($1,500) } . . . . **Note.** When figuring which amount is smaller, treat both amounts as positive numbers.	**21**	(	)
22 Do you have qualified dividends on Form 1040, line 9b? ☐ **Yes.** Complete Form 1040 through line 42, and then complete the **Qualified Dividends and Capital Gain Tax Worksheet** on page 37 of the Instructions for Form 1040. ☐ **No.** Complete the rest of Form 1040.			

Schedule D (Form 1040) 2004

chapter two:

Common AMT Adjustments

There are two adjustments that affect many individuals and will likely cause an individual taxpayer to pay an AMT. These adjustments are:

1. incentive stock options and
2. limitation on deductions.

Incentive Stock Options

The following case shows how significant the first adjustment dealing with *incentive stock options* can be.

Mr. Executive Case:

Jake Johnson has been retired for the past six months. He was recently notified that his tax liability was almost $100,000. His previous salary was in the 40's and his spouse's income is in the mid-30's.

Jake took early retirement and he exercised his right to buy incentive stock options that he had been awarded years before at a deep discount. The exercise was $1 and the share price was $90, resulting in an $89 gain per share.

To make matters worse, Jake only had a little over $100,000 in his 401(k) and IRAs. Personal bankruptcy will not discharge this $100,000 AMT liability, so Jake is stuck. He will have to rejoin the work force and his spouse will continue to work.

Do not confuse *incentive stock options* with numerous other types of incentive plans and stock options in general. Incentive stock option plans mean that the recipient employee can be granted the option (right to buy stock at a future date, *e.g.*, three years from the date of grant) and may exercise (buy) the stocks at that time with *no regular tax consequences*. The employee only pays regular tax on his or her Form 1040 when he or she actually sells the stock.

Not so with the AMT. The employee must include, as a positive adjustment to AMTI, on Line 13 of Form 6251 the excess, if any, of the following two items:

1. the fair market value of the stock acquired at the time of exercise of the option, when the employee's right first became transferable or no longer subject to forfeiture (*e.g.*, at end of holding period specified in option grant) ***over***
2. the amount the employee paid for the stock stated in the option (including any amount paid for the ISO, which is generally nothing).

This is the bargain element that is the AMT adjustment.

Example:

In Jake's case, he had an option price of $1 per share and the fair market value of the stock at the time of exercise was $90 per share. The positive AMT adjustment is $89 per share. If he had exercised options on 3,000 shares, his AMT adjustment would be $267,000 (3,000 shares x $89 per share).

Note: *Had Jake sold the 3,000 shares in the same year as he exercised the options, the tax treatment under the regular tax and the AMT would be identical. No AMT adjustment would be necessary, as he would have a regular tax liability based upon the $267,000. So, if you acquire stock by exercising an ISO and you dispose of that stock in the same year, the tax treatment under the regular tax and the AMT is the same—and no adjustment is required.*

Limitation on Deductions

This second adjustment, *limitation on deductions*, is actually a group of deductions made up of itemized and non-itemized deductions.

The itemized deductions are:

- Home Mortgage Interest (Line 4);
- Medical Expense (Line 2);
- Miscellaneous (Line 5); and,
- Taxes (state, local, etc.) (Line 3).

The nonitemized deductions are:

- Personal Exemption (instead of listing the personal exemptions as an adjustment on Form 6251, the form lists taxable income before the personal exemption deduction, Line 1);
- Standard Deduction (instead of listing the standard deduction as an adjustment on Form 6251, the form lists taxable income before the standard deduction, Line 6); and,
- Tax Refunds (these are attributable to state and local tax deductions, generally taken in earlier years, Line 7).

To understand the importance of the limitation of deductions adjustment, review the following cases.

CASE #1: Mr. and Mrs. Upwardly Mobile

The Turners are married with three young children. Both are employed. They earn a combined income of $150,000. Their state and local tax rate amounts to 8%, with $7,000 in real property taxes. They carry a $250,000 mortgage, with mortgage interest of $15,000. They also have a second mortgage (home equity loan) with $5,000 interest, used to pay credit card debt.

In 2003, they file their 1040, married filing jointly, and decrease their $150,000 of gross income by: five personal and dependency exemptions of $15,250, $15,000 mortgage interest, $5,000 home equity interest, $12,000 in state and local taxes, and $7,000 in real estate taxes. This results in a taxable income of $95,750, with a regular tax liability (before any withholding, credits, or estimated tax payments) of $18,064.

However, under the AMT, the Turners are not allowed deductions for state, local, and property taxes; interest on the home equity loan (unless for acquiring or improving existing residence); or, personal or dependency exemptions. They must *add back* to their taxable income of $95,750 the sum of $39,250 ($15,250 + $5,000 + $12,000 + $7,000). Their AMTI is $135,000, less the AMT exemption of $58,000, or $77,000. The $77,000 x .26 (AMT rate up to $175,000 AMTI), or $20,020, is their total tax liability.

Unfortunately for the Turners, their taxes have increased from a regular tax of $18,064 to $20,020 because of an AMT of $1,956. So, the Turners must pay a regular tax of $18,064 and an AMT of $1,956, for a total tax liability of $20,020.

CASE #2: Mr. & Mrs. Upper Class

Across the street from the Turners live the Andersons. Mr. and Mrs. Anderson have two children (one ready for college). In 2002, they filed married filing jointly with a combined income of $250,000, itemized deductions over $50,000, and state, local, and real property taxes of about $30,000. Their tax liability was approximately $55,000—with no AMT.

During 2003, however, things changed. The Andersons obtained a home equity loan (second mortgage) on their home to be used for their eldest child's college expenses. This resulted in additional interest of $5,000. They also purchased a vacation condo in Florida and watched their real property taxes increase by $10,000. Their total income for 2003 also increased to about $300,000 for the couple.

The $5,000 second mortgage interest, personal and dependency exemptions of $12,200, and $40,000 in state, local, and real property taxes all were denied under the AMT. The increases in nondeductible itemized deductions were sufficient to qualify the Andersons for the AMT in 2003. They owed an additional $8,500 in AMT to bring their 2003 tax liability to over $60,000.

CASE #3: Mr. and Mrs. Middle Class

The Carters have five children and file married filing jointly in 2003. Both are high school teachers and have a combined income of about $75,000. They presently rent and have taken the standard deduction of $9,500 in 2003.

Their regular tax bill liability is based on a taxable income of $44,150 ($75,000 gross income less ($9,500 standard deduction + $21,350 for seven personal and dependency exemptions)) for a regular tax liability in 2003 of $5,926 (before tax credits, withholding, or estimated tax).

The AMT, however, demands that the $44,150 of taxable income have the standard deduction and exemptions *added back*. So the AMTI is $75,000. This is reduced by their $58,000 AMT exemption, resulting in an AMT base of $17,000, for a total AMT of $4,420.

The Carters' regular tax liability of $5,926 exceeds the AMT amount of $4,420, so their total tax liability is the larger amount of $5,926.

CASE #4: Ms. Single Mom

Ms. Fisher is a single working mom. (Mr. Fisher died several years ago.) She has an income of $100,000 as a bank vice president, and files as head of household in 2003 because she is the sole support of her four young children. While there is no mortgage on the residence, she still has itemized deductions for state, local, and real property taxes of $15,000 (she resides in a high tax state), miscellaneous deductions of $4,000 (in excess of the 2% AGI limit), and deductible unreimbursed medical expenses of $5,500 (in excess of the 7.5% of AGI limit).

For regular tax, Ms. Fisher has a taxable income of $48,750 ($100,000 gross income less $36,000 itemized deductions and $15,250 personal and dependency exemptions), for a regular tax of $7,764 (before tax credits, withholding, and estimated tax).

The AMT requires that the following be *added back* to her taxable income of $48,750:

- state, local, real property taxes of $15,000;
- miscellaneous deductions of $4,000;
- unreimbursed medical expenses of $2,500 (The AMT allows a 10% limit on AGI and the regular tax only permits a 7.5% limit on AGI for unreimbursed medical expenses. Ms. Fisher must *add back* the smaller of 2.5% of AGI (2,500) or the medical expense deduction taken for regular tax ($5,500)); and,
- personal and dependency exemptions of $15,250.

This means that Ms. Fisher has an AMTI of $85,500 ($48,750 + 15,000 + 4,000 + 2,500 + 15,250), less the AMT exemption for head of household ($40,250). This results in an AMT base of $45,250 or an AMT liability of $11,765 ($45,250 x .26).

She must pay the greater of the regular tax ($7,764) and the AMT ($11,765). Therefore, her total tax liability will be $11,765—a regular tax of $7,764 plus an AMT of $4,001.

CASE #5: Mr. Retiree

Mr. Baxter is a healthy 70-year-old widower who still receives an annual taxable annuity of $50,000 from the sale of his business. He also receives an additional $50,000 in interest from fixed income investments.

He decided to take an Italian hiatus for eighteen months in Tuscany. He finances it by selling stock in 2003. The stock sale results in a capital gain of $75,000.

When he files as a single taxpayer in 2003, his AMT exemption of $40,250 is eliminated. The large capital gain of $75,000, when added to his other income of $100,000, exceeds the income limitation of $112,500.

Note: *While the tax rate on capital gains for both regular and AMT purposes is 15% (see Part III of Form 6251), the inclusion of the capital gains, and reduction or, in Mr. Baxter's case, elimination of the AMT exemption has the effect of raising this tax rate. Mr. Baxter pays capital gains of $11,250 and the additional AMT on the lost exemption of $40,250.*

Itemized Deductions

The adjustment known as the *limitation on deductions* is made up of limitations on *itemized deductions* and on *nonitemized deductions*. There are four broad categories of *itemized deductions* that are either reduced or eliminated from the AMT requiring that they be *added back* to taxable income to arrive at AMTI. Information about these itemized deductions (found on Schedule A) follow on the next page.

SCHEDULES A&B (Form 1040)

Department of the Treasury Internal Revenue Service (99)

Schedule A—Itemized Deductions

(Schedule B is on back)

▶ Attach to Form 1040. ▶ See Instructions for Schedules A and B (Form 1040).

OMB No. 1545-0074

2004

Attachment Sequence No. 07

Name(s) shown on Form 1040 | Your social security number

Section	Line	Description	Box	Amount
Medical and Dental Expenses		**Caution.** Do not include expenses reimbursed or paid by others.		
	1	Medical and dental expenses (see page A-2)	1	
	2	Enter amount from Form 1040, line 37 [2]		
	3	Multiply line 2 by 7.5% (.075)	3	
	4	Subtract line 3 from line 1. If line 3 is more than line 1, enter -0-		4
Taxes You Paid (See page A-2.)	5	State and local (check only one box): a ☐ Income taxes, or b ☐ General sales taxes (see page A-2)	5	
	6	Real estate taxes (see page A-3)	6	
	7	Personal property taxes	7	
	8	Other taxes. List type and amount ▶	8	
	9	Add lines 5 through 8		9
Interest You Paid (See page A-3.)	10	Home mortgage interest and points reported to you on Form 1098	10	
	11	Home mortgage interest not reported to you on Form 1098. If paid to the person from whom you bought the home, see page A-3 and show that person's name, identifying no., and address ▶	11	
Note. Personal interest is not deductible.	12	Points not reported to you on Form 1098. See page A-4 for special rules	12	
	13	Investment interest. Attach Form 4952 if required. (See page A-4.)	13	
	14	Add lines 10 through 13		14
Gifts to Charity If you made a gift and got a benefit for it, see page A-4.	15	Gifts by cash or check. If you made any gift of $250 or more, see page A-5	15	
	16	Other than by cash or check. If any gift of $250 or more, see page A-5. You **must** attach Form 8283 if over $500	16	
	17	Carryover from prior year	17	
	18	Add lines 15 through 17		18
Casualty and Theft Losses	19	Casualty or theft loss(es). Attach Form 4684. (See page A-5.)		19
Job Expenses and Most Other Miscellaneous Deductions (See page A-5.)	20	Unreimbursed employee expenses—job travel, union dues, job education, etc. Attach Form 2106 or 2106-EZ if required. (See page A-5.) ▶	20	
	21	Tax preparation fees	21	
	22	Other expenses—investment, safe deposit box, etc. List type and amount ▶	22	
	23	Add lines 20 through 22	23	
	24	Enter amount from Form 1040, line 37 [24]		
	25	Multiply line 24 by 2% (.02)	25	
	26	Subtract line 25 from line 23. If line 25 is more than line 23, enter -0-		26
Other Miscellaneous Deductions	27	Other—from list on page A-6. List type and amount ▶		27
Total Itemized Deductions	28	Is Form 1040, line 37, over $142,700 (over $71,350 if married filing separately)? ☐ **No.** Your deduction is not limited. Add the amounts in the far right column for lines 4 through 27. Also, enter this amount on Form 1040, line 39. ☐ **Yes.** Your deduction may be limited. See page A-6 for the amount to enter.	▶	28

For Paperwork Reduction Act Notice, see Form 1040 instructions. Cat. No. 11330X **Schedule A (Form 1040) 2004**

Interest

This is *home mortgage interest*, except for interest on a mortgage whose proceeds were used to buy, build, or improve the principal residence or a second home that is not used on a transient basis. It also excludes interest on a refinanced mortgage, but only to the extent that the refinanced amount did not exceed the balance of the mortgage immediately before the refinancing.

Example:

In Case #2, Mr. and Mrs. Anderson took a home equity loan and used the proceeds to assist in their eldest child's education. The interest on such a loan is deductible, up to $100,000, for regular tax purposes. However, unless the loan proceeds are used to acquire, construct, or improve the residence, no AMT deduction exists. The loan interest must be *added back* to their taxable income in order to compute AMTI.

If the Andersons had refinanced their mortgage to obtain the home equity portion and had applied it to remodeling their principal residence (and not their child's education), then the refinancing rule would apply. (The AMT interest deduction is limited to the balance of the mortgage immediately before the refinancing.)

For AMT purposes, had the Andersons refinanced an existing, original mortgage balance of $150,000 at 6% for a new mortgage of $200,000 at 3% in 2003, they could only deduct the interest on $150,000 of the refinanced loan. This was the outstanding principal balance immediately before the refinancing.

Note: *For practical IRS audit purposes, the taxpayer has the burden of proof. So be certain to keep all documentation of any home improvements.*

Medical Expenses

For regular tax purposes, *medical and dental expenses* are deductible to the extent they exceed 7.5% of *adjusted gross income* (AGI). But for AMT purposes, taxpayers must reduce their medical expenses further—to 10% of AGI. Consequently, taxpayers must *add back* to their taxable income the smaller of 2.5% of AGI (10% - 7.5%) or the medical expense deduction taken for regular tax purposes.

Example:

In Case #4, Ms. Fisher had unreimbursed medical expenses of $13,000, allowing her to deduct $5,500 for regular tax purposes ($13,000 - [.075 x $100,000]) and $3,000 allowed for AMT purposes ($13,000 - [.10 x $100,000]). So, she must add back $2,500 to taxable income to arrive at the allowable AMT medical expense deduction of $3,000 ($5,500 - $2,500), because this is smaller than the $5,500 regular tax medical expense deduction.

Note: *Employer, tax-advantaged health savings plan (for co-pays, deductibles, etc.) avoid both the regular tax and AMT floors. Consider participating in such tax-free plans if available.*

Health Savings Accounts (HSAs) are designed to help individuals save for qualified medical and retiree health expenses on a tax-free basis. Any individual who is covered by a high-deductible health plan may establish an HSA. Amounts contributed to an HSA belong to individuals and are completely portable. Every year, the money not spent stays in the account and gains interest, tax-free. For those that qualify, HSAs are a good way to take advantage of medical expenses that would otherwise not be deductible for either regular tax or AMT calculations.

Miscellaneous Deductions

Taxpayers have some confusion over whether any miscellaneous itemized deductions are allowed for AMT purposes. Here is an easy rule to remember: if the miscellaneous deduction is subject to a 2% of AGI floor, then the AMT does not recognize it. It must be *added back* to the taxable income as an adjustment. On the other hand, if it is a miscellaneous deduction not subject to the 2% of AGI floor, it is allowed for both regular tax and the AMT. No *add back* is necessary.

Some of the *typical* miscellaneous itemized deductions subject to the 2% of AGI floor include:

- appraisal fees;
- depreciation on home computer or cell phones used in business;
- fees to collect income, such as trust fees;
- hobby expenses (up to hobby income);
- investment fees and expenses;
- legal expenses (not personal in nature);
- loss on deposits;
- safe deposit box rental;
- tax preparation fees; and,

- unreimbursed employee expenses, such as:
    - employment agency fees;
    - job search fees;
    - license fees;
    - professional society dues;
    - résumé costs;
    - qualifying travel and transportation costs;
    - tools used in job; and,
    - uniforms and work clothes.

Some of the miscellaneous itemized deductions *not* subject to the 2% of AGI floor (and therefore deductible for both regular tax and the AMT) are:

- federal estate tax from income in respect of a decedent;
- gambling losses (up to gambling gains);
- income-producing property casualty and theft losses;
- impairment-related work expenses, such as physical or mental disability expenses attributable to attendant care, wheel chairs, etc.;
- premium on taxable bonds;
- repayments of amounts (greater than $3,000) previously included in income; and,
- tax-free return of annuity investment.

Example:

In Case #4, Ms. Fisher had excess miscellaneous deductions subject to the 2% of AGI floor of $4,000. If she also had a $2,000 impairment-related work expense during 2003 attributable to a special handicapped van service that assisted to and from her job while she had healing from an injury, these items would be reported for AMT purposes as follows:

- $4,000 *added back* to her taxable income for AMTI (because it was not allowed as deduction for AMT purposes) and
- $2,000 (entered on Line 27 or Schedule A) deductible for AMT purposes (because it was not subject to 2% of AGI floor and not added back to taxable income).

Note: *Each year the IRS publishes Publication 17, Your Federal Income Tax (For Individuals). It can be ordered from the IRS or downloaded and printed from the IRS website (**www.irs.gov**). It is free and very helpful in identifying miscellaneous deductions and other tax matters, such as changes in the tax law.*

One of the key tax-planning ideas in this area is to legitimately convert nondeductible (because of the 2% floor) or deductible (but subject to add back for AMT purposes) expenses into fully deductible items not subject to the 2% of AGI floor or the AMT *add back*.

This is accomplished by identifying possible *employee groups*. If you are a qualified performing artist, state or local official paid on a fee basis (*e.g.*, consultant), Armed Forces reservist traveling away from home, or an employee reimbursed for expenses, then such expenses are not subject to the 2% of AGI floor (regular tax) or required to be *added back* to taxable income for AMT purposes. These employees, therefore, avoid both the regular income tax and AMT limitations.

Taxes

Any state, local, income, or property tax (real estate, personal property as on a car or boat, etc.), foreign real property tax (tax on real estate on condo owned in Mexico), local and foreign income taxes, war profits, or excess profits taxes (rarely applicable to individual taxpayers), are not allowed for AMT purposes. Such taxes, while deductible as itemized deductions for the regular tax, must be *added back* to taxable income to arrive at AMTI.

Note: *On October 22, 2004, President Bush signed the American Jobs Creation Act of 2004. It made major changes in the corporate tax area. Included in the Act is a new tax provision that allows individuals to deduct, as an itemized deduction on Schedule A, their state sales taxes in place of their state income taxes for 2004 and 2005 only. Even taxpayers in the seven states with no state income tax (e.g., Florida, Texas, etc.) may deduct their state sales taxes.*

What does this new law mean for the AMT?

The same as with the state income tax itemized deduction, no such deduction is allowed for AMT purposes. So if you are subject to the AMT, it will result in no tax benefit.

Example:

In Case #1, the Turners' state and local income taxes of $12,000 and their real property taxes of $7,000 are shown as itemized deductions as their regular tax. However, they are not allowed for AMT purposes and are *added back* to their taxable income in order to compute AMTI.

To put the state, local, and property tax deductions in perspective, find your *per capita* 2002 state and local taxes as a percentage of personal (gross) income as calculated by the U.S. Department of Commerce. (see p.38.) Note the U.S. average.

Per Capita State and Local Tax

State	Percent	State	Percent
1. New York	13.11%	26. California	10.24%
2. Maine	12.83%	27. Montana	10.22%
3. Alaska	12.01%	28. Iowa	10.20%
4. Wisconsin	11.78%	29. Maryland	10.18%
5. Hawaii	11.53%	30. Washington	10.11%
6. New Mexico	11.38%	31. North Carolina	10.08%
7. Minnesota	11.30%	32. Georgia	10.05%
8. Wyoming	11.18%	33. Pennsylvania	10.04%
9. West Virginia	11.15%	34. Arkansas	10.03%
10. Rhode Island	11.14%	35. Illinois	10.01%
11. Utah	11.03%	36. Nevada	9.89%
12. North Dakota	11.00%	37. Oklahoma	9.87%
13. Vermont	10.97%	38. Idaho	9.82%
14. Michigan	10.89%	39. Massachusetts	9.52%
15. Ohio	10.79%	40. Virginia	9.35%
16. Louisiana	10.87%	41. Missouri	9.29%
17. Arizona	10.59%	42. Florida	9.15%
18. Delaware	10.53%	43. Colorado	9.14%
19. Connecticut	10.52%	44. Oregon	9.11%
20. Kentucky	10.51%	45. South Carolina	9.09%
21. Nebraska	10.45%	46. Alabama	9.07%
22. Mississippi	10.42%	47. Texas	9.04%
23. New Jersey	10.34%	48. South Dakota	8.95%
24. Kansas	10.31%	49. Tennessee	8.54%
25. Indiana	10.27%	50. New Hampshire	7.85%

U.S. Average 10.28%

In a similar vein, find your *per capita* 2002 local property taxes income as calculated by the U.S. Department of Commerce on the chart below. (Note, once again, the U.S. average.)

State	Dollars	State	Dollars
1. New Jersey	$1,716.88	26.Kansas	$790.44
2. Connecticut	1,587.63	27. Michigan	784.48
3. New York	1,328.09	28. Montana	763.98
4. Rhode Island	1,298.35	29. Georgia	718.73
5. New Hampshire	1,257.37	30. Arizona	703.35
6. Maine	1,229.78	31. California	676.21
7. Massachusetts	1,203.71	32. Nevada	672.94
8. Illinois	1,184.08	33. Idaho	670.07
9. Alaska	1,142.96	34. South Carolina	664.88
10. Wisconsin	1,044.41	35. Washington	643.85
11. Texas	950.37	36. Vermont	619.85
12. Minnesota	926.14	37. Missouri	605.28
13. Indiana	912.47	38. Utah	583.81
14. Nebraska	902.72	39. North Carolina	572.42
15. Iowa	888.35	40. Mississippi	513.40
16. Maryland	859.75	41. Tennessee	507.49
17. Colorado	855.57	42. Hawaii	497.22
18. Virginia	840.77	43. Delaware	487.87
19. Ohio	838.88	44. West Virginia	471.01
20. South Dakota	837.58	45. Louisiana	384.29
21. Florida	834.43	46. Oklahoma	377.46
22. Wyoming	832.78	47. Kentucky	329.78
23. North Dakota	817.10	48. New Mexico	321.93
24. Oregon	815.11	49. Alabama	260.92
25. Pennsylvania	810.12	50. Arkansas	180.98

U.S. Average 848.07

Example:

In 2002, an individual Illinois taxpayer with a gross income of $100,000 would have paid (and deducted as an itemized deduction), on average, $10,010 in state and local taxes ($100,000 x .1001) and $1,164.08 in local property taxes. This would be a combined tax deduction of $11,174.08. If you live in a high tax state (*e.g.*, California, New York, or Massachusetts), you are more severely punished than someone who lives in a low or no income tax state, such as Florida or Texas.

Nonitemized Deductions

There are three categories of nonitemized deductions.

Personal and Dependency Exemptions

No personal or dependency exemptions are allowed against the AMT. This means that all such exemption deductions must be *added back* to the taxable income to arrive at AMTI. Form 6251 does this for you. You will automatically exclude the personal and dependency exemptions by taking from Form 1040, either Line 40 (taxable income after itemized deductions, but before exemptions) or Line 37 (taxable income before both the standard deduction and exemption). Losing these exemptions makes a huge difference and often causes a person to pay the AMT. In Cases #1–#4, it worsened the situation for all taxpayers. But large families and single parents filing as heads of households are really penalized by this requirement.

Consider the following real-life case of Mr. and Mrs. Klaassen.

Case:

Mr. and Mrs. Klaassen were opposed to birth control and abortion. At the time they filed their 1994 tax return, as married filing jointly, they had ten children. (At the time of the case, they had thirteen.)

On their 1994 Form 1040, they reported twelve exemptions (two for themselves and ten for their children), reducing their taxable income by $29,400. (In 1994, each exemption had a value of $2,450.) In addition, they claimed medical and tax itemized deductions as $4,767.13 and $3,263.56, respectively.

They chose to completely ignore Form 6251, AMT. So they only reported that they owed a regular tax of $5,111 on their 1994 Form 1040.

Enter the IRS. A notice sent to the Klaassens in 1997 refigured their tax liability to include the AMT computation—adding back the $29,400 in disallowed personal and dependency exemptions.

Here is what the IRS did:

I. Individual Income Tax Return—Form 1040

Adjusted Gross Income	$83,056.42
Less: Itemized Deductions (Schedule A)	- $19,563.95
Balance	$63,492.47
Less: Exemptions	- $29,400.00
Taxable Income	$34,092.47
Regular Tax	$5,111.00

II. Itemized Expenses—Schedule A

Medical Expenses		
Actual Expenses	$10,996.36	
Less: 7.5% AGI	- $6,229.23	
Deductible amount		$4,767.13
State and Local Taxes		$3,263.56
Interest Paid		$3,585.76
Charitable Contributions		$7,947.50
Total Itemized Deductions		$19,563.95

III. Alternative Minimum Taxable Income

Taxable Income	$34,092.47
Adjustments	
Medical expenses (10% floor)*	$2,076.41
State and local taxes	$3,263.56
Exemptions	$29,400.00
Balance	$68,832.44
Plus: Items of Tax Preference	-0-
Alternative Minimum Taxable Income	$68,832.44

**The adjustment is computed as follows:*

Actual Medical Expenses	$10,996.36
Less: 10% AGI	- $8,305.64
AMT deductible amount	$2,690.72
Schedule A medical deduction	$4,767.13
Less: AMT deductible amount	- $2,690.72
Adjustment	$2,076.41

IV. Alternative Minimum Tax

Alternative Minimum Taxable Income	$68,832.44
Less: Exemption Amount	- $45,000.00
Taxable Excess	$23,832.44
Times: applicable AMT rate	x 26%
Tentative Minimum Tax	$6,196.43
Less: Regular Tax	- $5,111.00
Alternative Minimum Tax	$ 1,085.43

As you can see, the Klaassens owed an AMT of $1,085.43 in addition to their regular tax of $5,111, for a total tax liability of $6,196.43.

In U.S. Tax Court, the Klaassens argued that they were not liable for any AMT for two reasons. First, that the elimination of personal and dependency exemptions under the AMT adversely affects large families. Second, that taxpayers who choose large families for religious reasons have their First Amendment freedom of religion rights violated by the AMT.

In denying the validity of both arguments, the U.S. Tax Court found that the AMT statute was clear and precise with no room for interpretation.

Further, in its review of the First Amendment argument, it stated:

> *The fact that a law with a secular purpose may have the effect of making the observance of some religious beliefs more expensive does not render the statute unconstitutional under the First Amendment.*
>
> *Klaassen v. Commissioner, T.C. Memo 1998-241*

Standard Deduction

Another simple rule to remember is that, like the personal exemptions, *no* standard deduction is allowed for AMT purposes. Form 6251 picks up the taxable income before the standard deduction, so no *add back* calculation is necessary.

The basic rule for regular tax on Form 1040 is that a taxpayer will take the larger of the standard deduction or itemized deductions. The AMT may change this thinking.

Case of Mr. and Mrs. Snowbird

In 2003, Mr. and Mrs. Snowbird decided to move to Florida and enjoy the tax-free environment and sunny weather. When they filed their 2003 tax return in 2004, they discovered that the itemized deductions amounted to only $9,000, so they opted for the standard deduction of $9,500.

By opting for the standard deduction, they must *add back* to their AMT income the full $9,500, thereby creating a tax problem. If their lower itemized deductions comprised mortgage interest, charitable contributions, and miscellaneous deductions not subject to the 2% AGI floor, no AMT would result.

Mr. and Mrs. Snowbird could avoid this AMT trap by shifting some itemized deductions (*e.g.*, charitable contributions, prepaid mortgage interest, etc.) into 2003, which would exceed the standard deduction in 2003 of $9,500. Unfortunately, one cannot shift deductions *after* year end, so they would need to plan for this eventuality in the last quarter of 2003.

Note: *A taxpayer is allowed to claim either the standard deduction or itemized deductions, but is not required to select the greater in the tax law. Since certain itemized deductions can be used for the AMT, but the standard deduction cannot, itemizing may save you more money than taking the standard deduction, even when the standard deduction provides more of a savings for the regular tax. Be certain that if you opt for this, write "IE" (itemized elected) on Form 1040 on the line for itemized deductions.*

This provision becomes more important as the IRS continues to move toward a tax return-free system by 2007. Since the overwhelming majority of taxpayers take the standard deduction, which is indexed for inflation, they will need to find a way to make the election described in the example or they will be subjecting themselves to additional burdens of the AMT.

Tax Refunds

The regular tax allows an itemized deduction for state taxes paid. The AMT does not. So, a refund of overpaid state taxes in a following year will be included in the regular tax on Form 1040, but have no impact whatsoever on the AMT. However, if the taxpayer is self-employed and reduces his or her gross income to compute the AGI, then such a state tax refund *is* an adjustment to taxable income in computing the AMTI. If the refund is from state taxes originally deducted in arriving at AGI on Schedules C, E, or F, the refund is included on Form 6251 as a nonitemized deduction and increases AMTI.

Consider what might happen if a taxpayer wears two hats—one as an employee and one as a self-employed independent contractor. Now, add to the mix the fact that many taxpayers may pay state tax to two different states.

Example:

Brad works in New York as an editor (employee) at a New York publishing house. He also moonlights as a part-time magazine consultant (independent contractor) in New Jersey.

In 2003, he received two tax refunds—$1,000 from New York and $500 from New Jersey—for overpayment of taxes in 2002. But it is *where* he deducted the original state taxes in 2002 that controls how the tax refunds in 2003 are treated.

Brad did the following in 2002:

Schedule A, 1040	Schedule C, 1040
Deducted:	Deducted:
Itemized Expense	Business Expense
NY Tax $20,000	NJ Tax $1,500

So when he received the tax refunds in 2003, he correctly includes both ($1,000 New York and $500 New Jersey) in his gross income on the Form 1040. But on his Form 6251 for the AMT, only the $500 New Jersey tax refund increases his AMTI.

Why? Because Brad received an AMT deduction for the $1,500 New Jersey taxes in 2002. No such state tax deduction was allowed for the New York taxes, so the NY refund need not be included in AMT in 2003.

chapter three:

Unlikely AMT Adjustments

As the roadmap in Chapter 1 indicates, there are thirteen possible adjustments to the AMT. To put this in perspective, the Americans for Tax Reform estimates that by 2010, 85% of homeowners with two or more children and family incomes of at least $75,000 will need to pay the AMT. Understanding the adjustments will go a long way to reducing the likelihood that your family is in this group.

An AMT adjustment is capable of either increasing *or* decreasing your ultimate AMTI. The simplest way to view an adjustment is by comparing it to the volume control on your car radio. By touching the control, you either increase or decrease the volume. If that is clear, then you understand how the AMT adjustments work. Items that adjust your AMTI upward cause you to be more likely to pay AMT. Items that adjust your AMTI downward lower the amount you must pay or even eliminate your AMT liability.

For the sake of convenience, the thirteen adjustments are broken down into two groups—those that are most likely to be *used* by individual taxpayers, covered in this chapter, and those that are most likely to be *applied* by these taxpayers, covered in Chapter 3.

Of the thirteen adjustments, eleven are not likely to be applied to most taxpayers. It should come as no surprise that the lion's share of the adjustments will impact few individual, middle-class taxpayers. The AMT was originally designed to impact one in 500,000 taxpayers with annual incomes of at least $200,000 in 1969 dollars. That is at least $1,100,000 in annual income in 2004 dollars.

These adjustments, in alphabetical order (and where they are input on Form 6251) are:

- Alcohol Fuel Credit (Line 26);
- Basis Adjustment (Line 16);
- Circulation Costs (Line 20);
- Depreciation (Line 17);
- Installment Sales (Line 24);
- Long-Term Contracts (Line 21);
- Mining Costs (Line 22);
- Net Operating Loss (Lines 10, 27);
- Passive Activity Losses (Line 18);
- Pollution Control Facilities (Line 26); and,
- Tax Shelter Farm Activity (Line 26).

NA

Alcohol Fuel Credit

The *Alcohol Fuel Credit* is one of those adjustments that may affect taxpayers—noncorporate and corporate—albeit the latter really have greater interest. It is a tax credit (reduction of regular taxes dollar-for-dollar) for alcohol used in certain mixtures of gasoline, diesel fuel, etc., and is part of the *general business credit.* It is not recognized for AMT purposes. So, it does not apply when computing AMTI and is therefore a reduction to AMTI. Very few individual taxpayers, other than fuel producers or those in a trade or business as a fuel producer, are affected by this adjustment.

Basis Adjustment

Taxpayers—both corporate and noncorporate individuals—must adjust AMTI for the difference between any gain or loss for regular tax purposes (Schedule D, *Capital Gains and Losses*, Form 4684, *Casualties and Thefts*, and Form 4797, *Sales of Business Property*) and the AMT. Under the AMT calculation, a property's basis (cost) is reduced by the amount allowed as depreciation (cost recovery) *only*. Since other reductions may be allowed, including different depreciation methods for the regular tax, the adjusted basis (basis less depreciation adjustments) may be different.

An easy way to remember this adjustment is that you *must* compare apples to apples—not apples to oranges. So the gain or loss for AMTI must use the AMTI (not regular tax) basis.

Example:

Greg, a single individual, pays $15,000 for a new automobile in January, 2002. He intends to use it in his business. The AMT depreciation and regular tax depreciation are different each year, which means that the auto's tax basis also changes. This results in a problem when Greg sells the business auto at the end of 2003.

The tax basis of the business auto at the end of 2003 for AMT purposes is $9,855. (This is the original $15,000 cost, less AMT depreciation of $1,875 and $3,270 in years 2002 and 2003, respectively.) But that same tax basis for regular tax purposes is only $7,200. (This is the original $10,000 cost, less regular tax depreciation of $3,000 and $4,800, in the respective years of 2002 and 2003.)

If Greg sells the auto for $7,500 cash at the end of 2003, he experiences a $2,355 *loss* for AMT purposes and a $300 *gain* for regular tax purposes.

This suggests that the AMT may encourage a taxpayer to lease a business asset rather than purchase a business asset. In this example, the AMTI needs to be adjusted to reflect the difference between the $300 gain and the $2,355 loss—no such adjustment is necessary for leased business property.

Circulation Costs

Applicable as an adjustment to both corporate and noncorporate taxpayers, these are expenses to establish, maintain, or increase the *circulation* of a newspaper, magazine, or other periodical. Under the regular tax, these costs are deducted in the year paid or incurred. However, the AMT requires such costs to be written off over a three-year period. The difference between the regular tax and AMT deduction is an adjustment, and if the AMT deduction is greater, the entry is a negative amount that reduces AMTI. (Again, few individual taxpayers have this adjustment.)

Depreciation

As in the preceding three adjustments, both corporate and noncorporate individual taxpayers may be required to make a *depreciation* adjustment. A simple means of recalling this adjustment is that AMT calculations for depreciation require, in most cases, the use of the *alternative depreciation system* (ADS). Regular tax computations for depreciation demand, in most cases, the application of the *modified accelerated cost recovery system* (MACRS). Again, apples to apples.

The AMT-ADS method is basically a substitute for the regular tax MACRS method for real and personal property after 1986 and before 1999. Since you must use the AMT-ADS when figuring you AMT, there is an AMT adjustment. Luckily, the *Taxpayer Relief Act of 1997* somewhat simplified the adjustment. It applies to all property a taxpayer purchases and places in service after 1998.

Now, no adjustment for depreciation is necessary for AMT purposes if the property is real property depreciated on a straight-line basis. However, an adjustment for depreciation may be required if the property is personal property. The AMT-ADS method uses a 150% declining balance method in 2004, whereas the regular tax MACRS employs a 200% declining balance method.

Example:

Peter, a single individual, purchases and places into service a $20,000 automobile for use in his business. The auto has a 5-year life. His AMT adjustments for the period are as follows:

Year	Regular Tax—MACRS *(200% Adjustment)*	AMT-ADS *(150% Adjustment)*	AMT—Depreciation Adjustment
2004	$4,000	$3,000	$1,000
2005	6,400	5,100	1,300
2006	3,840	3,570	270
2007	2,304	3,332	<1,028>
2008	2,304	3,332	<1,028>
2009	1,152	1,666	<514>
	$20,000	$20,000	$-0-

Peter must increase AMTI in the first three years and decrease it in the last three years.

These earlier year increases in AMTI can be reduced with business asset purchases that throw off negative adjustments in years 2004 through 2006, like the car will in years 2007 through 2009. Had this asset base been real property (*e.g.*, an easement interest), no adjustment would be required.

Installment Sales

An *installment sales* adjustment only applies to nondealers (individual sales) in personal property and to dispositions of farm property. After 1987, there is generally no AMT adjustment for installment sales. However, chances are that because of the ability of the individual, nondealer taxpayer to defer the reporting of income, the adjusted basis of the property sold will be different for regular tax versus the AMT. Such a difference may trigger a basis adjustment in the year of sale, as described earlier in this section. (Few individual taxpayers need be concerned with this adjustment.)

Long-Term Contracts

When a taxpayer enters into a contract that is not completed within the taxable year it was entered into (for example, a building, installation, construction, or manufacturing contract), then special rules are triggered. Since both regular tax and the AMT recognize the *percentage-of-completion method* (in which the contract price is reported as income in proportion to the part of the contract completed during the taxable year), there is no adjustment.

However, taxpayers who chose to use a form of completed contract (in which the contract price is reported as income in the taxable year of completion) or other deferral method must make an adjustment. For AMT purposes, the excess of deferred income over the regular tax percentage of completion must be included as a positive adjustment to AMTI. So, for example, if in a five-year, one million dollar deferred contract, no income is reported until the fifth year, the AMT adjustment would be 20% (assuming proportional costs), or $200,000 positive AMT adjustment each year.

N/A

Mining Costs

Like circulation costs, mining costs are applicable to both corporate and noncorporate taxpayers. Regular tax allows their immediate deduction in the year paid or incurred, whereas the AMT requires a ten-year write-off of such costs. When the AMT mining cost deduction is greater, AMTI has a negative adjustment, and vice versa.

Net Operating Loss

Equally applicable to both corporate and noncorporate taxpayers is the *net operating loss* (NOL)—excess of allowable deductions over gross income from a trade or business. For regular tax purposes, it virtually guarantees that no tax is due from the taxpayer, as the tax base is negative. Common sense dictates that if the regular tax NOL (on Form 1040, Schedule C for individuals or Form 1120 for corporations) were allowed to be *carried over* onto Form 6251, it could have a similar effect and wipe out any AMT liability in that year. To prevent that, the regular tax NOL must be adjusted for AMT purposes. It cannot offset more than 90% of AMTI. This ensures that a taxpayer with no regular tax liability will pay some AMT, thus, a measure of fairness in the tax system.

The NOL deduction is entered twice on Form 6251. Once as a positive adjustment to AMTI on Line 10, and then as a recomputed *alternative tax NOL deduction* (ATNOLD) on Line 27. This latter NOL deduction (ATNOLD) is the sum of the AMT-NOL carryovers and carrybacks from prior and future years to this tax year. The

AMT-NOL is the excess of AMT deductions for AMTI (ignoring ATNOLD) over the income included in AMTI. A special calculation, known as the *ATNOLD limitation*, needs to be made and Line 27 reflects the smaller of the ATNOLD or the ATNOLD limitation. (For the few affected individual taxpayers, Form 6251 instructions should be reviewed.)

Passive Activity Losses

The period when tax shelters were commonly allowing $10 to $1 write-offs came to a crashing halt with the 1986 *Tax Reform Act*. There, a new category of losses, known as *passive activity losses* (PALs) spelled the end of these excessive noneconomic losses. A passive activity is an activity that involves the conduct of any trade or business in which the taxpayer does not materially participate. For example, a rental activity is presumed to be passive in most cases.

Only taxpayers who are individuals, estates, trusts, closely-held C corporations, and personal service corporations need make the AMT adjustment for PALs. The regular tax rules generally control how the AMT-PALs adjustment is computed. To make the computation, taxpayers with passive activities need to do the following.

- Review all Schedule K-1 (Form 1065) and other tax documents that set forth the PALs.
- Determine whether any other items for AMT purposes are not allowed.

- Recalculate the PALs using Form 8582, *Passive Activity Loss Limitations.*
- Enter the recalculated AMT-PAL on the appropriate schedule (C, E, F, or Form 4835, *Farm Rental Income and Expenses*). Determine if the AMT-PAL loss exceeds the regular tax loss. If it does, then you enter the adjustment as a negative number on Line 18 of Form 6251.

Example:

As a passive partner in a partnership, you receive a Schedule K-1 that shows the following:

a. PAL: $4,125
b. Depreciation adjustment (post-1986): $500
c. Property disposition adjustment: $225

Since b and c are not allowed as AMT adjustments, the PAL is reduced by these amounts resulting in an AMT-PAL of $3,400.

$4,125 - $500 - $225 = $3,400

Form 8852 is then completed, compared with regular tax loss on Schedule C, E, F, or Form 4835, and the PAL adjustment is then recorded on Form 6251, Line 18.

n/a

Pollution Control Facilities

For regular tax purposes, both corporate and noncorporate taxpayers may elect to use the five-year (60 month) write off of pollution control facilities. No such provision is available for AMT purposes. For years after 1998, the write off of such facilities for AMT purposes uses the regular MACRS depreciation with the straight-line method. If the AMT amount exceeds the regular tax, a negative adjustment is made to AMTI. (Few individual taxpayers are affected by this adjustment.)

Form **8582**

Department of the Treasury
Internal Revenue Service (99)

Passive Activity Loss Limitations

▶ See separate instructions.
▶ Attach to Form 1040 or Form 1041.

OMB No. 1545-1008
2004
Attachment Sequence No. **88**

Name(s) shown on return | Identifying number

Part I **2004 Passive Activity Loss**
Caution: *See the instructions for Worksheets 1, 2, and 3 on pages 7 and 8 before completing Part I.*

Rental Real Estate Activities With Active Participation (For the definition of active participation see **Special Allowance for Rental Real Estate Activities** on page 3 of the instructions.)

1a Activities with net income (enter the amount from Worksheet 1, column (a))	1a		
b Activities with net loss (enter the amount from Worksheet 1, column (b))	1b	( )	
c Prior years unallowed losses (enter the amount from Worksheet 1, column (c))	1c	( )	
d Combine lines 1a, 1b, and 1c			1d

Commercial Revitalization Deductions From Rental Real Estate Activities

2a Commercial revitalization deductions from Worksheet 2, column (a)	2a	( )	
b Prior year unallowed commercial revitalization deductions from Worksheet 2, column (b)	2b	( )	
c Add lines 2a and 2b			2c ( )

All Other Passive Activities

3a Activities with net income (enter the amount from Worksheet 3, column (a))	3a		
b Activities with net loss (enter the amount from Worksheet 3, column (b))	3b	( )	
c Prior years unallowed losses (enter the amount from Worksheet 3, column (c))	3c	( )	
d Combine lines 3a, 3b, and 3c			3d

4 Combine lines 1d, 2c, and 3d. If the result is net income or zero, all losses are allowed, including any prior year unallowed losses entered on line 1c, 2b, or 3c. **Do not** complete Form 8582. Report the losses on the forms and schedules normally used . . . **4**

If line 4 is a loss and:
- Line 1d is a loss, go to Part II.
- Line 2c is a loss (and line 1d is zero or more), skip Part II and go to Part III.
- Line 3d is a loss (and lines 1d and 2c are zero or more), skip Parts II and III and go to line 15.

Caution: *If your filing status is married filing separately and you lived with your spouse at any time during the year,* ***do not*** *complete Part II or Part III. Instead, go to line 15.*

Part II **Special Allowance for Rental Real Estate With Active Participation**
Note: *Enter all numbers in Part II as positive amounts. See page 8 for an example.*

5 Enter the **smaller** of the loss on line 1d or the loss on line 4			5
6 Enter $150,000. If married filing separately, see page 8	6		
7 Enter modified adjusted gross income, but not less than zero (see page 8)	7		
Note: *If line 7 is greater than or equal to line 6, skip lines 8 and 9, enter -0- on line 10. Otherwise, go to line 8.*			
8 Subtract line 7 from line 6	8		
9 Multiply line 8 by 50% (.5). **Do not** enter more than $25,000. If married filing separately, see page 8			9
10 Enter the **smaller** of line 5 or line 9			10

If line 2c is a loss, go to Part III. Otherwise, go to line 15.

Part III **Special Allowance for Commercial Revitalization Deductions From Rental Real Estate Activities**
Note: *Enter all numbers in Part III as positive amounts. See the example for Part II on page 8.*

11 Enter $25,000 reduced by the amount, if any, on line 10. If married filing separately, see instructions	11
12 Enter the loss from line 4	12
13 Reduce line 12 by the amount on line 10	13
14 Enter the **smallest** of line 2c (treated as a positive amount), line 11, or line 13	14

Part IV **Total Losses Allowed**

15 Add the income, if any, on lines 1a and 3a and enter the total	15
16 **Total losses allowed from all passive activities for 2004.** Add lines 10, 14, and 15. See pages 10 and 11 of the instructions to find out how to report the losses on your tax return	16

For Paperwork Reduction Act Notice, see page 12 of the instructions. Cat. No. 63704F Form **8582** (2004)

Form 8582 (2004) Page 2

Caution: *The worksheets must be filed with your tax return. Keep a copy for your records.*

Worksheet 1—For Form 8582, Lines 1a, 1b, and 1c (See page 7 of the instructions.)

Name of activity	Current year		Prior years	Overall gain or loss	
	(a) Net income (line 1a)	(b) Net loss (line 1b)	(c) Unallowed loss (line 1c)	(d) Gain	(e) Loss
Total. Enter on Form 8582, lines 1a, 1b, and 1c . . . . ▶					

Worksheet 2—For Form 8582, Lines 2a and 2b (See pages 7 and 8 of the instructions.)

Name of activity	(a) Current year deductions (line 2a)	(b) Prior year unallowed deductions (line 2b)	(c) Overall loss
Total. Enter on Form 8582, lines 2a and 2b . . . . ▶			

Worksheet 3—For Form 8582, Lines 3a, 3b, and 3c (See page 8 of the instructions.)

Name of activity	Current year		Prior years	Overall gain or loss	
	(a) Net income (line 3a)	(b) Net loss (line 3b)	(c) Unallowed loss (line 3c)	(d) Gain	(e) Loss
Total. Enter on Form 8582, lines 3a, 3b, and 3c . . . . ▶					

Worksheet 4—Use this worksheet if an amount is shown on Form 8582, line 10 or 14 (See page 9.)

Name of activity	Form or schedule and line number to be reported on (see instructions)	(a) Loss	(b) Ratio	(c) Special allowance	(d) Subtract column (c) from column (a)
Total . . . . ▶			1.00		

Worksheet 5—Allocation of Unallowed Losses (See page 9 of the instructions.)

Name of activity	Form or schedule and line number to be reported on (see instructions)	(a) Loss	(b) Ratio	(c) Unallowed loss
Total . . . . ▶			1.00	

Form **8582** (2004)

Form 8582 (2004) Page **3**

Worksheet 6—Allowed Losses (See pages 9 and 10 of the instructions.)

Name of activity	Form or schedule and line number to be reported on (see instructions)	(a) Loss	(b) Unallowed loss	(c) Allowed loss
Total . . . . ▶				

Worksheet 7—Activities With Losses Reported on Two or More Different Forms or Schedules (See page 10.)

Name of Activity:	(a)	(b)	(c) Ratio	(d) Unallowed loss	(e) Allowed loss
Form or schedule and line number to be reported on (see instructions):					
1a Net loss plus prior year unallowed loss from form or schedule . . ▶					
b Net income from form or schedule . . . . ▶					
c Subtract line 1b from line 1a. If zero or less, enter -0- ▶					
Form or schedule and line number to be reported on (see instructions):					
1a Net loss plus prior year unallowed loss from form or schedule . . ▶					
b Net income from form or schedule . . . . ▶					
c Subtract line 1b from line 1a. If zero or less, enter -0- ▶					
Form or schedule and line number to be reported on (see instructions):					
1a Net loss plus prior year unallowed loss from form or schedule . . ▶					
b Net income from form or schedule . . . . ▶					
c Subtract line 1b from line 1a. If zero or less, enter -0- ▶					
Total . . . . ▶			1.00		

Printed on recycled paper

Form **8582** (2004)

Tax Shelter Farm Activity

Individual taxpayers who have a gain or loss from a tax shelter farm activity (such as a farming syndicate) that is not a passive activity will recalculate the tax shelter farm activity. This occurs by taking into account any AMT adjustments and preferences, much like with PALs. If the tax shelter farm activity is from a passive activity (*i.e.*, not a farming syndicate), then it is recalculated and included with the other PALs on Form 6251, Line 18.

Adjustments carry with them the opportunity to plan around them by accelerating or deferring certain regular tax deductions. With that in mind, an adjustment can increase or decrease AMTI. Go back and review all thirteen adjustments discussed in these past two chapters. Keep in mind that your situation changes every year, as does the amount of any adjustments.

chapter four: Tax Preference Items

In the last two chapters, thirteen different adjustments were discussed. The purpose of this chapter is to review the five *tax preference items* (TPIs) and see how they might affect the individual taxpayer. An item of tax preference (tax preference item or TPI) is any one of a series of deductions or preferentially treated income under the AMT. While adjustments can either increase or decrease AMTI, TPIs can only increase AMTI. It is this difference that casts emphasis on TPIs, but impacts few *individual* taxpayers.

The five TPIs (in alphabetical order and where they are found on Form 6251) are:

1. Accelerated Depreciation (pre-1987) (Line 26);
2. Depletion (Line 9);
3. Intangible Drilling Costs (Line 25);
4. Small Business Stock Exclusion (Line 12); and,
5. Tax-Exempt Interest (Line 11).

The nature of TPIs is vastly different for the average, middle-class taxpayer than the character of the adjustments. While all taxpayers who file take the standard deduction or itemize and claim personal exemptions, few have tax-exempt bonds, oil and gas properties, or pre-1987 (in 2004) depreciable properties.

TPIs are to be avoided at all costs because they can only put a taxpayer in a worse AMT position. While tax planning is vital for both adjustments and TPIs, the latter, if left unchecked, can create real havoc to a taxpayer's AMT liability.

TPIs are applicable to both individual and corporate taxpayers, but only two (or possibly three) of the TPIs have any real significance for individuals. These are accelerated depreciation, small business stock exclusion, and the most important, tax-exempt interest.

Accelerated Depreciation (pre-1987)

If you purchased and placed in service property *before* 1987, then the depreciation on real property that *exceeds* the property's straight-line depreciation is a TPI. Similarly, if you purchased and placed in service certified pollution control facilities (unlikely for individual taxpayers), then the amortization that exceeds the facilities sixty-month rate is a TPI. (This accelerated depreciation TPI is rarely a problem for taxpayers.)

Note: *Even if the TPI is applicable, a negative TPI cannot be used to reduce AMTI.*

Example:

Charlie, a retiree, placed real property in service in 1985. It had a 15-year accelerated cost recovery system (ACRS) recovery period. (ACRS did not become MACRS until the 1986 Tax Reform Act.) In 1986, the ACRS accelerated depreciation was *more* than the straight-line depreciation, and the excess had to be treated as a TPI increasing AMTI. But in 1992, when ACRS accelerated depreciation was *less* than straight-line depreciation, there is no TPI and AMTI remains unchanged.

Depletion

A special provision for the extractive industries (mining, oil and gas, etc.) exists. It is known as *percentage depletion.* This oil depletion allowance lets taxpayers with oil and gas interests count as income only 87.5% of their royalties from such interests. However, with the AMT, the *excess* of the percentage depletion allowance (tax deduction for regular tax purposes) over the property's adjusted basis is a TPI and increases AMTI. (Few individual taxpayers are concerned with this TPI.)

Note: *Most of the taxpayers who take this deduction are not individuals, but are other entities, such as oil and gas partnerships, trusts, etc.*

Intangible Drilling Costs

To provide an economic incentive for the extractive industries to take the risk associated with drilling for oil, the tax law allows a special regular tax deduction, the *intangible drilling costs deduction* (IDC), for drilling costs on oil, gas, and geothermal wells. For AMT purposes, the TPI for such drilling costs is measured by the *excess* IDC that are greater than 65% of the well's (property's) net income. And the excess IDC are merely those regular tax deduction IDC over the amortized cost for 120 months. (Again, few taxpayers face this TPI. However, those that do should consult the instructions to Form 6251.)

Small Business Stock Exclusion

The economic lifeblood of this country is small business and the entrepreneurial spirit. To foster this continued growth of small business, Congress granted a special regular tax exclusion (not a deduction) on the gain a taxpayer has on *small business stock*.

There is substantial confusion, even among highly educated CPAs, lawyers, bankers, etc., as to what the terms exemption, exclusion, deduction, and credit mean in the tax area. The following should prove helpful.

- **Exemptions** are special deductions that allow certain classes of income or taxpayers to pay no tax (*e.g.*, personal and dependency exemptions).
- **Exclusions** are specific classes of income or taxpayers that need not be included in income or pay tax, respectively (*e.g.*, receipt of a Christmas gift).
- **Deductions** are always based on what Congress and the tax law say. In general terms, a deduction is an expense paid in cash, in kind, or claimed on paper that reduces taxable income. However, unlike a tax credit, the value of a tax deduction is directly measured by your marginal tax bracket. For instance, if you decide to give $1,000 to your church for its building campaign and your tax bracket is 35%, your out-of-pocket cost is $650 (tax deduction x (1 - tax rate)). Uncle Sam lets you deduct against your taxable income on Form 1040, Schedule A, "Itemized Deductions," the $1,000 charitable deduction. Notice that the higher a taxpayer's marginal tax bracket, the more valuable the deduction.
- **Credits** are amounts that offset, dollar-for-dollar, tax liability. Deductions only reduce taxable income. They do not directly lower your tax liability. Tax credits are either **refundable** (reduction in tax liability may become a negative amount, for example, earned income credit or credit for withholding on wages) or **nonrefundable** (reduction in tax liability cannot be reduced below $0, for example, foreign tax credit or minimum tax credit). Tax credits are more valuable than tax deductions and are not based upon a taxpayer's marginal tax bracket.

It is crucial that you understand exactly what is considered small business stock, as it is given a very specific definition in the tax law. It means stock issued after August 10, 1993, by a C corporation that has at least 80% of its assets invested in its active business. Its total assets, at the time it issues the stock, cannot exceed $50 million.

Once you know that the stock you have sold qualifies as small business stock, then for regular tax (Form 1040) purposes you are allowed to *exclude* (not deduct) 50% of the gain on the sale or exchange, provided you held the stock for more than five years.

Unfortunately, the AMT-TPI treatment is not as straightforward. Two different TPI rules existed in 2003. Select the one that covers your situation when you sold the small business stock.

Rule No. 1

If you sold or exchanged qualified small business stock *before* May 6, 2003, multiply the excluded gain (Schedule D, *Capital Gains and Losses*) by 42%.

Rule No. 2

If you sold or exchanged qualified small business stock *after* May 5, 2003, multiply the excluded gain (Schedule D, *Capital Gains and Losses*) by 7%.

Note: *Since Rule No. 2 will only apply to post May 5, 2003, sales or exchanges of small business stock, taxpayers will be applying this rule in 2004 and future years. This is a softening of the TPI from 42% to 7%. In other words, the* *actual amount of gain used to increase AMTI is only 3.5% (7% of the 50% regular tax exclusion).*

Example:

In 2004, Joseph sold qualified small business stock that he held since 1995. His taxable gain was $100,000. He may exclude $50,000 (.50 x $100,000) for regular tax purposes. On Form 6251, however, he must include (as a TPI) 7% of the excluded gain or $3,500 (.07 x $50,000). Notice, this is 3.5% of his total gain.

Tax-Exempt Interest

Countless retirees seek to achieve a balance in their portfolios by trading off greater risk in stocks for greater security in bonds. In addition to retirees, wealthy taxpayers seek out municipal bonds that bear tax-exempt interest. Not only are such bonds generally exempt from federal income taxes, but the state issuer usually exempts it from that state's income taxes. For instance, in the high-tax state of New York, it is possible to find a New York state bond (MUNI) exempt from both federal and New York state tax.

MUNIs and PABs

MUNIs can be issued for governmental or nongovernmental purposes. If they are issued for nongovernmental purposes, a potential exists for them to be reclassified as a *private activity bond* (PAB).

A PAB is a municipal bond in which more than 10% of the bond proceeds will be used in a private activity (a business), and more than 10% of the interest paid will be secured by property used in a private activity or obtained from a private activity. To make matters worse, interest on PABs (with exceptions) is to be treated as a TPI.

Example:

The State of Florida wants to attract a private international air carrier firm, XYZ Carriers, Inc., to Orlando International Airport. To cement the deal, the State of Florida will float a bond issue to build new hangars, runways, and other facilities for XYZ, using approximately 40% of the monies raised from the bond issue. The remainder will be used for state roads and access to the airport. Such bonds meet the definition of a PAB.

If your MUNI bond is reclassified as a PAB, you *lose* the regular tax benefit (interest exclusion from gross income) unless the PAB is a *qualified* bond. If a PAB is a *qualified* (also called *specified* after the *1986 Tax Reform Act*) bond, it meets further requirements dealing with use of proceeds, etc. (Examples of such bonds are qualified mortgage bonds, student loan bonds, redevelopment bonds, 501(c)(3) (charitable organization) bonds, etc.)

Confusing? To a bondholder, the difference between a PAB and a MUNI is akin to a duck. If it walks, quacks, and flies like a duck, then it is a duck. However, this is not so with PABs.

These *animals* are identified on Wall Street as bonds—IOUs—whose proceeds are used to finance nongovernmental activities. Though issued as part of a state or local bond issue, it is not a *pure* MUNI. How do you know you have got a real duck and not a decoy? *Always* review the bond prospectus (required to be issued by the municipality). It will tell you whether it is a PAB or a true MUNI.

But why do only PABs trigger an AMT?

Because Congress felt that such MUNIs were not true MUNIs (the proceeds of which were used to benefit the private sector). So there is no tax break for the AMT when you receive interest from such a bond. After all, it is not a true MUNI (duck) but only a PAB (decoy).

Generally, a taxpayer-investor will buy a MUNI thinking it is *completely* tax free—the interest is tax exempt for regular and AMT purposes. The following rules will be helpful to remember whenever a municipal bond is purchased.

Rule No. 1

First, not all PABs are tax exempt for regular tax (Form 1040) purposes. If the PAB is not tax exempt for regular tax, then there is no TPI on the tax exempt interest. The interest is already included in taxable income and goes into the AMTI.

Rule No. 2

Second, only qualified PABs trigger a TPI. Such MUNIs, issued after the 1986 *Tax Reform Act*, are easy to identify because they will be truly *tax exempt* bonds allowing for an interest exclusion from taxable income.

Rule No. 3

Third, any borrowings to buy or carry such qualified PABs will have interest payments. But the regular tax law specifically denies any deduction for this interest. Not so the AMT. The AMT allows the interest expense you incur if you borrow money to buy qualified PABs to reduce the gain you receive from the PABs.

Example:

Mike borrowed funds from his credit union to buy a qualified tax exempt PAB. The PAB pays him $20,000 in interest and he pays the credit union $10,000 in interest. For regular tax purposes in 2003, Mike has no interest income of $20,000 (it is a qualified PAB) and no interest tax deduction of $10,000. However, for AMT purposes on Form 6251, Line 11, he shows a net TPI of $10,000 ($20,000 exempt interest less $10,000 credit union interest expense).

Rule No. 4

Last, on Form 6251, Line 8, there is an adjustment that applies to individual taxpayers called *investment interest expense. Investment interest* (affecting certain individual taxpayers, such as retirees, high income individuals, etc.) is any interest allowed as a regular tax deduction on debt from *investment* property.

Note: *The special home mortgage interest adjustment rules (Form 6251, Line 4) are discussed in Chapter 2.*

For regular tax purposes, investment interest is only deductible up to the amount of investment income. Any excess interest over income may be carried over to future tax years.

Example:

In 2004, Virginia paid $17,000 of investment interest and received $15,000 of investment income. Only $15,000 of investment interest can be used to offset the $15,000 of investment income in 2004. The remaining $2,000 of investment interest is carried forward to be used in 2005 and future taxable years.

This investment interest rule is of concern because the AMT rule follows the regular tax rule and affects PABs. Here is what you want to remember about qualified PABs.

- Their interest is a TPI.
- As Rule No. 3 indicates, expenses, including interest, for purchasing or carrying the qualified PABs are deductible—*but only for AMT purposes.* The use of Line 8 is to show the *difference* between the qualified PABs interest and deductions for regular tax versus the AMT.

Example:

In 2003, Sarah has net investment income and investment interest expense from corporate bonds of $70,000 and $50,000, respectively. She also has interest income and interest expenses from qualified PABs of $40,000 and $60,000, respectively.

For regular tax (Form 1040) purposes, she has an investment interest deduction of $50,000 (the PAB interest expense is nondeductible). For AMT (Form 6251, Line 8) purposes, she has an interest deduction of $110,000 ($50,000 + $60,000 as both interest expenses are deductible). As for the net investment income, Sarah will show for AMT purposes $110,000 ($70,000 regular tax net investment income + $40,000 interest income from PABs). This means that she can deduct the full $110,000 of interest expense for AMT purposes because it is equal to the net investment income.

Note: *In addition to the treatment of qualified PABs under the investment interest rule, there are special categories of elections (tax choices you make each year based on your situation). Form 4952, Investment Interest Expense Deduction, should be completed for the PABs and these special capital gain and qualified dividend elections. It will be filed with Form 6251.*

Form **4952** | **Investment Interest Expense Deduction** | OMB No. 1545-0191 **2004**

Department of the Treasury Internal Revenue Service (99) | ▶ **Attach to your tax return.** | Attachment Sequence No. **12B**

Name(s) shown on return | **Identifying number**

Part I Total Investment Interest Expense

1	Investment interest expense paid or accrued in 2004 (see instructions)	1	
2	Disallowed investment interest expense from 2003 Form 4952, line 7	2	
3	**Total investment interest expense.** Add lines 1 and 2	3	

Part II Net Investment Income

4a	Gross income from property held for investment (excluding any net gain from the disposition of property held for investment)	4a			
b	Qualified dividends included on line 4a	4b			
c	Subtract line 4b from line 4a			4c	
d	Net gain from the disposition of property held for investment	4d			
e	Enter the **smaller** of line 4d or your net capital gain from the disposition of property held for investment (see instructions)	4e			
f	Subtract line 4e from line 4d			4f	
g	Enter the amount from lines 4b and 4e that you elect to include in investment income (see instructions)			4g	
h	Investment income. Add lines 4c, 4f, and 4g			4h	
5	Investment expenses (see instructions)			5	
6	**Net investment income.** Subtract line 5 from line 4h. If zero or less, enter -0-			6	

Part III Investment Interest Expense Deduction

7	Disallowed investment interest expense to be carried forward to 2005. Subtract line 6 from line 3. If zero or less, enter -0-	7	
8	**Investment interest expense deduction.** Enter the **smaller** of line 3 or 6. See instructions.	8	

Section references are to the Internal Revenue Code unless otherwise noted.

General Instructions

Purpose of Form

Use Form 4952 to figure the amount of investment interest expense you can deduct for 2004 and the amount you can carry forward to future years. Your investment interest expense deduction is limited to your net investment income.

For more information, see Pub. 550, Investment Income and Expenses.

Who Must File

If you are an individual, estate, or a trust, you must file Form 4952 to claim a deduction for your investment interest expense.

Exception. You do not have to file Form 4952 if all of the following apply.

- Your investment interest expense is not more than your investment income from interest and ordinary dividends minus any qualified dividends.
- You have no other deductible investment expenses.
- You have no disallowed investment interest expense from 2003.

Allocation of Interest Expense

If you paid or accrued interest on a loan and used the loan proceeds for more than one purpose, you may have to allocate the interest. This is necessary because different rules apply to investment interest, personal interest, trade or business interest, home mortgage interest, and passive activity interest. See Pub. 535, Business Expenses.

Specific Instructions

Part I—Total Investment Interest Expense

Line 1

Enter the investment interest expense paid or accrued during the tax year, regardless of when you incurred the indebtedness. Investment interest expense is interest paid or accrued on a loan or part of a loan that is allocable to property held for investment (as defined on this page).

Include investment interest expense reported to you on Schedule K-1 from a partnership or an S corporation. Include amortization of bond premium on taxable bonds purchased after October 22, 1986, but before January 1, 1988, unless you elected to offset amortizable bond premium against the interest payments on the bond. A taxable bond is a bond on which the interest is includible in gross income.

Investment interest expense does not include any of the following:

- Home mortgage interest.
- Interest expense that is properly allocable to a passive activity. Generally, a passive activity is any business activity in which you do not materially participate and any rental activity. See the Instructions for Form 8582, Passive Activity Loss Limitations, for details.
- Any interest expense that is capitalized, such as construction interest subject to section 263A.
- Interest expense related to tax-exempt interest income under section 265.
- Interest expense, disallowed under section 264, on indebtedness with respect to life insurance, endowment, or annuity contracts issued after June 8, 1997, even if the proceeds were used to purchase any property held for investment.

Property held for investment. Property held for investment includes property that produces income, not derived in the ordinary course of a trade or business, from interest, dividends, annuities, or royalties. It also includes property that produces gain or loss, not derived in the ordinary course of a trade or business, from the disposition of property that produces these types of income or is held for investment. However, it does not include an interest in a passive activity.

Exception. A working interest in an oil or gas property that you held directly or through an entity that did not limit your liability is property held for investment, but only if you did not materially participate in the activity.

Part II—Net Investment Income

Line 4a

Gross income from property held for investment includes income, unless derived in the ordinary course of a trade or business, from interest, ordinary dividends (except Alaska Permanent Fund dividends) annuities, and royalties.

Identifying a Qualified PAB

Once you have these four basic rules under your belt, the next item of importance is to be capable of identifying, in the marketplace, a qualified PAB. Taxpayer-investors buy qualified PABs (MUNIs) either as separate bonds or, more likely, as bond funds.

Note: *To identify municipal bond funds, including the new AMT bond funds, it is wise to review their performance. In this regard, see* ***www.morningstar.com****. See also* ***www.touchstoneinvestments.com*** *for an example of an AMT municipal bond fund. For an excellent website to gain further understanding of MUNIs, see* ***www.investinginbonds.com****, sponsored by the Bond Market Association.*

Perhaps the easiest means of identifying a qualified PAB is to review the prospectus or official statement that accompanies the bond offering (assuming the bond is bought in the primary market). It must state therein, usually under *tax consequences* or the like, the true nature of the PAB. Another means, albeit after-the-fact, is to look at the sales confirmation that identifies the type of bond you purchased. In the case of a MUNI bond fund, the fund's prospectus describes and identifies the kind of bonds and, most importantly, the percentage of the MUNIs in the fund that will be qualified PABs.

With the added AMT exposure and risk, these qualified PABs (interest excluded for regular tax but treated as a TPI for AMT) will command a higher yield.

And remember, if it sounds too good to be true, it probably is! Check out the bond or the final fund before you buy.

Provided your sales representative is knowledgeable and ethical, and you review the materials beforehand, these monies may be an answer to paying less regular tax and some AMT. With proper AMT planning, this TPI can be substantially reduced.

chapter five: Importance of the AMT Credits

No discussion of AMT would be complete without a review of tax credits and the all-important minimum tax credit. As discussed earlier, tax credits are dollar-for-dollar reduction in taxes. A $1,000 income tax credit directly reduces your income tax liability by $1,000. The purpose of this chapter is to identify the allowable tax credits and, most importantly, the use of the *minimum tax credit* (MTC).

For individual taxpayers, few regular tax credits carry over to reduce the AMT. The rule of thumb is that the more tax credits claimed for regular tax purposes (reducing your regular tax to zero, or in some cases, a refund), the more likely that you will pay an AMT. One of the bedrock principles of the AMT is that tax credits, which can virtually wipe the slate clean for regular tax purposes, should never do the same for the AMT.

For AMT purposes there are two major classifications of tax credits. One is *nonrefundable personal credits* and the other is the *foreign tax credit*.

Nonrefundable Personal Credits

As a result of the 2004 *Working Families Tax Relief Act*, nonrefundable personal credits (dependent care credit, credit for the elderly and permanently and totally disabled, mortgage credit, child tax credit, Hope and Lifetime Learning credits, adoption credits, saver's credit, and the DC homebuyer credit) are allowed *in total* against *both* regular tax and the AMT for tax years 2004 and 2005.

In 2006 (unless Congress chooses to make this permanent), only the child tax credit, elective deferrals and IRA contributions credit, and the adoption expense credit will be allowed against the AMT.

Even with this change, however, the combined total of nonrefundable personal credits is limited to the sum of the regular tax liability (reduced by the foreign tax credit) and the AMT.

N/A

Foreign Tax Credit

Other than the nonrefundable personal tax credits, the only remaining allowable tax credit for individual taxpayers is the *foreign tax credit* (FTC). This credit must be computed separately for AMT purposes and is commonly referred to as the AMTFTC. It is so complex in its calculations that taxpayers expecting to have this credit should review Publication 514, *Foreign Tax Credit for Individuals* and review the instructions for Form 1116, *Foreign Tax Credit*. (You can find both at **www.irs.gov**.) The following is a brief, general description of what an individual taxpayer is attempting to accomplish by using the AMTFTC.

Example:

Donna takes her dream job in Paris. As a senior editor of a fashion magazine, she earns $100,000 of income in France (in U.S. dollars). Since she is still a U.S. citizen, she must pay tax on her total worldwide income. So she includes the $100,000 on her Form 1040 NR (nonresident) and pays tax at 35%, or $35,000.

Unfortunately, France also taxes the $100,000 at 35%. So she now has paid 70% of her income to two jurisdictions—the U.S. and France. In an effort to alleviate this unfair result, individual taxpayers are allowed to exclude for regular tax and AMT purposes up to $80,000 of foreign earned income. So now Donna includes only $20,000 of her income. However, she is still paying tax at 35% to both the U.S. and France on the $20,000.

To relieve the taxpayer of this double taxation, Congress created a tax credit. The foreign tax credit is a dollar-for-dollar reduction of U.S. tax for tax paid to a foreign country. In this case, the $7,000 of U.S. taxes (.35 x $20,000) would be offset by the $7,000 (.35 x $20,000) of French taxes.

You can decide not to take the U.S. foreign tax credit, but in most cases, a dollar-for-dollar offset of U.S. taxes beats a deduction that may only offset U.S. taxes by 35 cents for every dollar deducted (assuming the taxpayer is in the 35% tax bracket).

Form **1116**

Department of the Treasury
Internal Revenue Service

Foreign Tax Credit

(Individual, Estate, or Trust)

▶ **Attach to Form 1040, 1040NR, 1041, or 990-T.**

▶ **See separate instructions.**

OMB No. 1545-0121

2004

Attachment Sequence No. **19**

Name | **Identifying number** as shown on page 1 of your tax return

Use a separate Form 1116 for each category of income listed below. See **Categories of Income** on page 3 of the instructions. Check only one box on each Form 1116. Report all amounts in U.S. dollars except where specified in Part II below.

a ☐ Passive income
b ☐ High withholding tax interest
c ☐ Financial services income
d ☐ Shipping income
e ☐ Dividends from a DISC or former DISC
f ☐ Certain distributions from a foreign sales corporation (FSC) or former FSC
g ☐ Lump-sum distributions
h ☐ Section 901(j) income
i ☐ Certain income re-sourced by treaty
j ☐ General limitation income

k Resident of (name of country) ▶

Note: *If you paid taxes to only one foreign country or U.S. possession, use column A in Part I and line A in Part II. If you paid taxes to* ***more than one*** *foreign country or U.S. possession, use a separate column and line for each country or possession.*

Part I Taxable Income or Loss From Sources Outside the United States (for Category Checked Above)

	Foreign Country or U.S. Possession			Total
	A	B	C	(Add cols. A, B, and C.)
I **Enter the name of the foreign country or U.S. possession** ▶				
1 Gross income from sources within country shown above and of the type checked above (see page 7 of the instructions):				1
Deductions and losses (***Caution:*** *See pages 9, 11, and 12 of the instructions*):				
2 Expenses **definitely related** to the income on line 1 (attach statement)				
3 Pro rata share of other deductions **not definitely related:**				
a Certain itemized deductions or standard deduction (see instructions)				
b Other deductions (attach statement)				
c Add lines 3a and 3b				
d Gross foreign source income (see instructions)				
e Gross income from all sources (see instructions)				
f Divide line 3d by line 3e (see instructions)				
g Multiply line 3c by line 3f				
4 Pro rata share of interest expense (see instructions):				
a Home mortgage interest (use worksheet on page 12 of the instructions)				
b Other interest expense				
5 Losses from foreign sources				
6 Add lines 2, 3g, 4a, 4b, and 5				6
7 Subtract line 6 from line 1. Enter the result here and on line 14, page 2 ▶				7

Part II Foreign Taxes Paid or Accrued (see page 12 of the instructions)

Country	Credit is claimed for taxes (you must check one) (m) ☐ Paid (n) ☐ Accrued	Foreign taxes paid or accrued								
		In foreign currency				In U.S. dollars				
		Taxes withheld at source on:			(s) Other foreign taxes paid or accrued	Taxes withheld at source on:			(w) Other foreign taxes paid or accrued	(x) Total foreign taxes paid or accrued (add cols. (t) through (w))
	(o) Date paid or accrued	(p) Dividends	(q) Rents and royalties	(r) Interest		(t) Dividends	(u) Rents and royalties	(v) Interest		
A										
B										
C										

8 Add lines A through C, column (x). Enter the total here and on line 9, page 2 ▶ 8

For Paperwork Reduction Act Notice, see page 16 of the instructions. Cat. No. 11440U Form **1116** (2004)

Form 1116 (2004) Page **2**

Part III **Figuring the Credit**

9	Enter the amount from line 8. These are your total foreign taxes paid or accrued for the category of income checked above Part I	9	
10	Carryback or carryover (attach detailed computation)	10	
11	Add lines 9 and 10	11	
12	Reduction in foreign taxes (see page 13 of the instructions)	12	
13	Subtract line 12 from line 11. This is the total amount of foreign taxes available for credit	13	
14	Enter the amount from line 7. This is your taxable income or (loss) from sources outside the United States (before adjustments) for the category of income checked above Part I (see page 14 of the instructions)	14	
15	Adjustments to line 14 (see page 14 of the instructions)	15	
16	Combine the amounts on lines 14 and 15. This is your net foreign source taxable income. (If the result is zero or less, you have no foreign tax credit for the category of income you checked above Part I. Skip lines 17 through 21. However, if you are filing more than one Form 1116, you must complete line 19.)	16	
17	**Individuals:** Enter the amount from Form 1040, line 40. If you are a nonresident alien, enter the amount from Form 1040NR, line 37. **Estates and trusts:** Enter your taxable income without the deduction for your exemption	17	
	Caution: *If you figured your tax using the lower rates on qualified dividends or capital gains, see page 15 of the instructions.*		
18	Divide line 16 by line 17. If line 16 is more than line 17, enter "1"	18	
19	**Individuals:** Enter the amount from Form 1040, line 43, **less** any amounts on Form 1040, lines 46 through 49. If you are a nonresident alien, enter the amount from Form 1040NR, line 40, **less** any amounts on Form 1040NR, lines 43 and 44. **Estates and trusts:** Enter the amount from Form 1041, Schedule G, line 1a, or the total of Form 990-T, lines 36 and 37	19	
	Caution: *If you are completing line 19 for separate category* ***g*** *(lump-sum distributions), see page 16 of the instructions.*		
20	Multiply line 19 by line 18 (maximum amount of credit)	20	
21	Enter the **smaller** of line 13 or line 20. If this is the only Form 1116 you are filing, skip lines 22 through 30 and enter this amount on line 31. Otherwise, complete the appropriate line in Part IV (see page 16 of the instructions) ▶	21	

Part IV **Summary of Credits From Separate Parts III** (see page 16 of the instructions)

22	Credit for taxes on passive income	22	
23	Credit for taxes on high withholding tax interest	23	
24	Credit for taxes on financial services income	24	
25	Credit for taxes on shipping income	25	
26	Credit for taxes on dividends from a DISC or former DISC and certain distributions from a FSC or former FSC	26	
27	Credit for taxes on lump-sum distributions	27	
28	Credit for taxes on certain income re-sourced by treaty	28	
29	Credit for taxes on general limitation income	29	
30	Add lines 22 through 29	30	
31	Enter the **smaller** of line 19 or line 30	31	
32	Reduction of credit for international boycott operations. See instructions for line 12 on page 14	32	
33	Subtract line 32 from line 31. This is your **foreign tax credit.** Enter here and on Form 1040, line 50; Form 1040NR, line 45; Form 1041, Schedule G, line 2a; or Form 990-T, line 40a ▶	33	

Printed on recycled paper

Form **1116** (2004)

Form **1040NR** Department of the Treasury Internal Revenue Service

U.S. Nonresident Alien Income Tax Return

For the year January 1–December 31, 2004, or other tax year beginning , 2004, and ending , 20

OMB No. 1545-0089

2004

Please print or type.

Your first name and initial	Last name	**Identifying number (see page 7 of inst.)**
Present home address (number, street, and apt. no., or rural route). If you have a P.O. box, see page 7.		Check if: ☐ Individual ☐ Estate or Trust
City, town or post office, state, and ZIP code. If you have a foreign address, see page 7.		**For Disclosure and Paperwork Reduction Act Notice, see page 27.**
Country ▶	Of what country were you a **citizen** or national during the tax year? ▶	
Give address **outside the United States** to which you want any refund check mailed. If same as above, write "Same."	Give address in the country where you are a **permanent resident.** If same as above, write "Same."	

Attach Forms W-2 here. Also attach Form(s) 1099-R if tax was withheld.

Filing Status and Exemptions for Individuals (see page 7)

Filing status. Check only one box (1–6 below).

		7a Yourself	7b Spouse
1	☐ Single resident of Canada or Mexico, or a single U.S. national		
2	☐ Other single nonresident alien		
3	☐ Married resident of Canada or Mexico, or a married U.S. national — If you check box 7b, enter your spouse's identifying number ▶		
4	☐ Married resident of Japan or the Republic of Korea		
5	☐ Other married nonresident alien		
6	☐ Qualifying widow(er) with dependent child (see page 7)		

Caution: ***Do not*** *check box 7a if your parent (or someone else) can claim you as a dependent.* ***Do not*** *check box 7b if your spouse had any U.S. gross income.*

No. of boxes checked on 7a and 7b ▶ ____

7c **Dependents:** (see page 8) (1) First name Last name	(2) Dependent's identifying number	(3) Dependent's relationship to you	(4) ✓ if qualifying child for child tax credit (see page 8)
			☐
			☐
			☐
			☐

No. of children on 7c who:
lived with you ▶ ____
did not live with you due to divorce or separation ▶ ____
Dependents on 7c not entered above ▶ ____

d Total number of exemptions claimed — **Add numbers entered on lines above** ▶ ☐

Enclose, but do not attach, any payment.

Income Effectively Connected With U.S. Trade/Business

8	Wages, salaries, tips, etc. Attach Form(s) W-2		8
9a	**Taxable** interest		9a
b	**Tax-exempt** interest. **Do not** include on line 9a	9b	
10a	Ordinary dividends		10a
b	Qualified dividends (see page 10)	10b	
11	Taxable refunds, credits, or offsets of state and local income taxes (see page 10)		11
12	Scholarship and fellowship grants. Attach Form(s) 1042-S or required statement (see page 10)		12
13	Business income or (loss). Attach Schedule C or C-EZ (Form 1040)		13
14	Capital gain or (loss). Attach Schedule D (Form 1040) if required. If not required, check here ☐		14
15	Other gains or (losses). Attach Form 4797		15
16a	Total IRA distributions — 16a — **16b** Taxable amount (see page 11)		16b
17a	Pensions and annuities — 17a — **17b** Taxable amount (see page 11)		17b
18	Rental real estate, royalties, partnerships, trusts, etc. Attach Schedule E (Form 1040)		18
19	Farm income or (loss). Attach Schedule F (Form 1040)		19
20	Unemployment compensation		20
21	Other income. List type and amount (see page 13)		21
22	Total income exempt by a treaty from page 5, Item M	22	
23	Add lines 8, 9a, 10a, 11–15, 16b, and 17b–21. This is your **total effectively connected income** ▶		23

Adjusted Gross Income

24	Deduction for clean-fuel vehicles (see page 13)	24	
25	IRA deduction (see page 14)	25	
26	Student loan interest deduction (see page 14)	26	
27	Health savings account deduction. Attach Form 8889	27	
28	Moving expenses. Attach Form 3903	28	
29	Self-employed health insurance deduction (see page 14)	29	
30	Self-employed SEP, SIMPLE, and qualified plans	30	
31	Penalty on early withdrawal of savings	31	
32	Scholarship and fellowship grants excluded	32	
33	Add lines 24 through 32		33
34	Subtract line 33 from line 23. Enter here and on line 35. This is your **adjusted gross income** ▶		34

Cat. No. 11364D

Form **1040NR** (2004)

Form 1040NR (2004) Page **2**

Section	Line	Description	Box	
Tax and Credits	35	Amount from line 34 (adjusted gross income)	35	
	36	**Itemized deductions** from page 3, Schedule A, line 17	36	
	37	Subtract line 36 from line 35	37	
	38	Exemptions (see page 15)	38	
	39	**Taxable income.** Subtract line 38 from line 37. If line 38 is more than line 37, enter -0-	39	
	40	**Tax** (see page 16). Check if any tax is from: a ☐ Form(s) 8814 b ☐ Form 4972	40	
	41	**Alternative minimum tax** (see page 16). Attach Form 6251	41	
	42	Add lines 40 and 41 ▶	42	
	43	Credit for child and dependent care expenses. Attach Form 2441	43	
	44	Credits from: a ☐ Form 8396 b ☐ Form 8859	44	
	45	Foreign tax credit. Attach Form 1116 if required	45	
	46	Child tax credit (see page 18)	46	
	47	Retirement savings contributions credit. Attach Form 8880	47	
	48	Adoption credit. Attach Form 8839	48	
	49	Other credits. Check applicable box(es): a ☐ Form 3800 b ☐ Form 8801 c ☐ Form (specify)	49	
	50	Add lines 43 through 49. These are your **total credits**	50	
	51	Subtract line 50 from line 42. If line 50 is more than line 42, enter -0- ▶	51	
Other Taxes	52	Tax on income not effectively connected with a U.S. trade or business from page 4, line 87	52	
	53	Social security and Medicare tax on tip income not reported to employer. Attach Form 4137	53	
	54	Additional tax on IRAs, other qualified retirement plans, etc. Attach Form 5329 if required	54	
	55	Transportation tax (see page 19)	55	
	56	Household employment taxes. Attach Schedule H (Form 1040)	56	
	57	Add lines 51 through 56. This is your **total tax** ▶	57	
Payments	58	Federal income tax withheld from Forms W-2, 1099, 1042-S, etc.	58	
	59	2004 estimated tax payments and amount applied from 2003 return	59	
	60	Excess social security and tier 1 RRTA tax withheld (see page 20)	60	
	61	Additional child tax credit. Attach Form 8812	61	
	62	Amount paid with Form 4868 (request for extension)	62	
	63	Other payments from: a ☐ Form 2439 b ☐ Form 4136 c ☐ Form 8885	63	
	64	Credit for amount paid with Form 1040-C	64	
	65	U.S. tax withheld at source from page 4, line 84	65	
	66	U.S. tax withheld at source by partnerships under section 1446:		
	a	From Form(s) 8805	66a	
	b	From Form(s) 1042-S	66b	
	67	U.S. tax withheld on dispositions of U.S. real property interests:		
	a	From Form(s) 8288-A	67a	
	b	From Form(s) 1042-S	67b	
	68	Add lines 58 through 67b. These are your **total payments** ▶	68	
Refund Direct deposit? See page 21.	69	If line 68 is more than line 57, subtract line 57 from line 68. This is the amount you **overpaid**	69	
	70a	Amount of line 69 you want **refunded to you.**	70a	
	b	Routing number ▶ c Type: ☐ Checking ☐ Savings		
	d	Account number		
	71	Amount of line 69 you want **applied to your 2005 estimated tax** ▶	71	
Amount You Owe	72	Amount you owe. Subtract line 68 from line 57. For details on how to pay, see page 21 ▶	72	
	73	Estimated tax penalty. Also include on line 72	73	

Third Party Designee — Do you want to allow another person to discuss this return with the IRS (see page 22)? ☐ **Yes.** Complete the following. ☐ **No**

Designee's name ▶ Phone no. ▶ ( ) Personal identification number (PIN) ▶

Sign Here — Keep a copy of this return for your records.

Under penalties of perjury, I declare that I have examined this return and accompanying schedules and statements, and to the best of my knowledge and belief, they are true, correct, and complete. Declaration of preparer (other than taxpayer) is based on all information of which preparer has any knowledge.

Your signature ▶	Date	Your occupation in the United States

Paid Preparer's Use Only

Preparer's signature ▶	Date	Check if self-employed ☐	Preparer's SSN or PTIN
Firm's name (or yours if self-employed), address, and ZIP code ▶		EIN	
		Phone no. ( )	

Form **1040NR** (2004)

N/A

Foreign Tax Credit Limitation

The FTC would be complicated by itself *without* any limitations on it. But Congress chose to impose limitations on the FTC for *both* regular tax and the AMT. This limitation is designed to prevent foreign taxes from reducing U.S. taxes on U.S. income. Simply stated, the FTC limitation limits the FTC to foreign income taxes on foreign source income to the extent those taxes do *not* exceed the U.S. taxes on that foreign source income.

Example:

Ramon works as an engineer all over the world. He has a five-year contract in Brazil, but travels to the U.S. and will not qualify for the $80,000 exclusion of foreign earned income. He receives $150,000 in Brazil (which has a 50% tax rate) and another $200,000 from U.S. companies as a field engineer. His U.S. income is taxed at 35%.

Ramon's worldwide taxable income reported on the Form 1040 NR is $350,000. U.S. taxes on this income is $122,500 (.35 x $350,000). His Brazilian income is $150,000, which results in a Brazilian tax of $75,000 (.50 x $150,000).

If he uses the FTC and offsets the U.S. tax of $122,500 with the Brazilian tax of $75,000, his net U.S. tax liability is $47,500, or an effective tax rate of only 23.75% ($47,500/$200,000). By using the FTC, Ramon is able to lower his 35% U.S. tax rate on U.S. income to less than 24%, for a savings of over 11%.

Generally, this regular tax FTC limitation can be put into an equation:

$$\frac{X}{\text{U.S. income tax}} = \frac{\text{Foreign source income}}{\text{Worldwide taxable income}}$$

If we place Ramon from the previous example within this limitation, here is what happens:

$$\frac{X}{\$122{,}500} = \frac{\$150{,}000}{\$350{,}000}$$

Solving for X (amount of foreign taxes that can be credited that taxable year against U.S. taxes), results in a figure of $52,500. This means that for the current taxable year, only $52,500 of the $75,000 in foreign (Brazilian) taxes can be used as a FTC against U.S. taxes. U.S. taxes of $122,500 offset by $52,500 of Brazilian taxes produces a net U.S. tax liability of $70,000, or an effective tax rate on U.S. source income of 35% ($70,000/$200,000).

AMTFTC Limitation

Once the regular tax FTC limitation and credit is computed, it must be recalculated for the AMT. As a result of the *American Jobs Creation Act of 2004*, it has become somewhat easier to compute. Now the amount of foreign taxes paid on U.S. source AMT income is calculated with its limitation to arrive at the amount used as a foreign tax credit against U.S. AMTI.

Prior to January 1, 2005, one had to *readjust* the AMTFTC by 90% of the AMT. This is no longer the case. Now the *full* amount of AMTFTC computed is allowed, just like the regular tax FTC computation. This thereby abolishes the 90% limitation.

Note: *The unused AMTFTC may be carried back one year and carried forward ten years.*

Minimum Tax Credit

Much of life is timing. Tax computation is no different. Because of timing differences produced, for instance, by depreciation adjustments under the regular tax versus the AMT, the payment of an AMT in one year and a regular tax in another needed to be made fair to taxpayers. The mechanism used to smooth out these timing differences is known as the *minimum tax credit* (MTC).

The MTC is designed to recognize the fact that taxpayers may receive no tax deferral under the AMT for numerous transactions, (accelerated depreciation, installment sales, etc.) that produce an AMT liability. Given this fact, the MTC will compensate a taxpayer who loses a regular tax benefit in one year by allowing that same taxpayer to reduce his or her regular tax liability by the amount of the MTC in future taxable years. So under this credit, a taxpayer's AMT is allowed as a credit against regular tax liability in the future.

Basically, an MTC occurs whenever you paid an AMT in an earlier year because of *deferral items*. Deferral items are AMT adjustments that *reverse* in future years—for example, depreciation. Taking depreciation on an accelerated basis for regular tax versus the AMT results in a timing difference that *corrects* itself in future years. The following is a list of the deferral items that trigger a MTC.

- *Circulation Costs* (expensed for regular tax, but amortized for three years for AMT)
- *Post-1986 Depreciation* (either general or alternate depreciation for regular tax, but only alternate for AMT)
- *Property Dispositions* (must recalculate gain or loss for AMT because of basis differences)
- *Incentive Stock Options* (not a taxable event upon exercise for regular tax, but *is* generally taxable for AMT)
- *Installment Sales* (nondealers may use for regular tax between August 16, 1986 and January 1, 1987; not so for AMT)
- *Intangible Drilling Costs* (expense or amortize over sixty months for regular tax, but generally 120 months for AMT)
- *Long-term Contracts* (regular tax requires percentage completion with exceptions; none for AMT)
- *Loss Limitations* (limited to at-risk for regular tax; recalculate for AMT)
- *Mining Costs* (expense or amortize for 120 months for regular tax, but must be amortized for 120 months for AMT)

- *Passive Activity Losses* (limited to passive income for regular tax; recalculated for AMT)
- *Research and Development Costs* (expensed or amortized for regular tax but must be amortized over 120 months for AMT)

Example:

In 1998, Julie places a tangible asset in service that had $8,000 of regular tax depreciation and $5,000 of AMT depreciation, triggering the AMT liability. Five years later, she had $1,000 of regular tax depreciation and $3,500 of AMT depreciation, resulting in a regular tax liability. Without the MTC, a double taxation on the same income can result.

Computing the MTC

The MTC is computed as the difference between the AMT computed with exclusion and deferral items and the AMT computed using only exclusion items. It is computed only on deferral (timing difference) items. Exclusion amounts are not allowed in the MTC computation. Such exclusion items include adjustment for miscellaneous itemized deductions, certain taxes, depletion TPI, tax-exempt interest TPI, and the small business stock exclusion TPI.

Because of the numerous changes that can occur from year to year for a taxpayer, it is very important that separate records be kept to track the MTC. The carryforward lasts until the date of death of the taxpayer, so tracking it is important.

It is wise to always file Form 8801, *Credit For Prior Year Minimum Tax—Individuals, Estates and Trusts* and review the two page Instructions that accompany Form 8801. It is easy to forget about the credit as years pass. Form 8801 serves as another reminder.

Form 8801 has two parts. Part I, Net Minimum Tax on Exclusion Items, is used to compute the AMT adjustments that do not reverse in a future year, commonly referred to as *permanent changes*. Such exclusion items are:

- Home Mortgage Interest;
- Depletion;
- Interest from Private Activity Bonds;
- Investment Internet Expenses;
- Medical and Dental Expenses;
- Miscellaneous Deductions;
- Qualified Small Business Stock;
- Tax Refunds; and,
- Taxes.

Part II, MTC and Carryforward, is the end result of computing the MTC on deferral items. MTC carryovers increase this figure and any MTC not allowed in the current year are carried forward indefinitely.

Filing the Form 8801 as suggested by the IRS will document and establish your MTC and any carryovers.

With the understanding of the components of and calculations for determining the AMT, you are now prepared to venture into some AMT planning. But first, spend a few moments scanning the preceding chapters to refresh your memory on the AMT roadmap, thirteen adjustments, tax preference items, and tax credits (including the MTC).

Form **8801**

Department of the Treasury
Internal Revenue Service (99)

Credit for Prior Year Minimum Tax— Individuals, Estates, and Trusts

▶ See instructions on pages 3 and 4.
▶ Attach to Form 1040, 1040NR, or 1041.

OMB No. 1545-1073
2004
Attachment Sequence No. **74**

Name(s) shown on return	Identifying number

Part I Net Minimum Tax on Exclusion Items

1	Combine lines 1, 6, and 10 of your 2003 Form 6251. Estates and trusts, see instructions	1	
2	Enter adjustments and preferences treated as exclusion items (see instructions)	2	
3	Minimum tax credit net operating loss deduction (see instructions)	3	( )
4	Combine lines 1, 2, and 3. If zero or less, enter -0- here and on line 15 and go to Part II. If more than $191,000 and you were married filing separately for 2003, see instructions	4	
5	Enter: $58,000 if married filing jointly or qualifying widow(er) for 2003; $40,250 if single or head of household for 2003; or $29,000 if married filing separately for 2003. Estates and trusts, enter $22,500	5	
6	Enter: $150,000 if married filing jointly or qualifying widow(er) for 2003; $112,500 if single or head of household for 2003; or $75,000 if married filing separately for 2003. Estates and trusts, enter $75,000	6	
7	Subtract line 6 from line 4. If zero or less, enter -0- here and on line 8 and go to line 9	7	
8	Multiply line 7 by 25% (.25)	8	
9	Subtract line 8 from line 5. If zero or less, enter -0-. If this form is for a child under age 14, see instructions	9	
10	Subtract line 9 from line 4. If zero or less, enter -0- here and on line 15 and go to Part II. Form 1040NR filers, see instructions	10	
11	• If **for 2003** you reported capital gain distributions directly on Form 1040, line 13a; you reported qualified dividends on Form 1040, line 9b (Form 1041, line 2b(2); **or** you had a gain on both lines 16 and 17a of Schedule D (Form 1040) (lines 15a and 16a, column (2), of Schedule D (Form 1041)), complete Part III of Form 8801 and enter the amount from line 56 here. • **All others:** If line 10 is $175,000 or less ($87,500 or less if married filing separately for 2003), multiply line 10 by 26% (.26). Otherwise, multiply line 10 by 28% (.28) and subtract $3,500 ($1,750 if married filing separately for 2003) from the result.	11	
12	Minimum tax foreign tax credit on exclusion items (see instructions)	12	
13	Tentative minimum tax on exclusion items. Subtract line 12 from line 11	13	
14	Enter the amount from your 2003 Form 6251, line 34, or 2003 Form 1041, Schedule I, line 55	14	
15	**Net minimum tax on exclusion items.** Subtract line 14 from line 13. If zero or less, enter -0-	15	

Part II Minimum Tax Credit and Carryforward to 2005

16	Enter the amount from your 2003 Form 6251, line 35, or 2003 Form 1041, Schedule I, line 56	16	
17	Enter the amount from line 15 above	17	
18	Subtract line 17 from line 16. If less than zero, enter as a negative amount	18	
19	**2003 minimum tax credit carryforward.** Enter the amount from your 2003 Form 8801, line 26	19	
20	Enter the total of your 2003 unallowed nonconventional source fuel credit and 2003 unallowed qualified electric vehicle credit (see instructions)	20	
21	Combine lines 18, 19, and 20. If zero or less, **stop here** and see instructions	21	
22	Enter your 2004 regular income tax liability minus allowable credits (see instructions)	22	
23	Enter the amount from your 2004 Form 6251, line 33, or 2004 Form 1041, Schedule I, line 54	23	
24	Subtract line 23 from line 22. If zero or less, enter -0-	24	
25	**Minimum tax credit.** Enter the **smaller** of line 21 or line 24. Also enter this amount on your 2004 Form 1040, line 54; Form 1040NR, line 49; or Form 1041, Schedule G, line 2d	25	
26	**Minimum tax credit carryforward to 2005.** Subtract line 25 from line 21. Keep a record of this amount because you may use it in future years	26	

For Paperwork Reduction Act Notice, see page 4. Cat. No. 10002S Form **8801** (2004)

Form 8801 (2004) Page **2**

Part III **Tax Computation Using Maximum Capital Gains Rates**

Caution: *If you did not complete Part IV of the 2003 Schedule D (Form 1040) (or Part V of the 2003 Schedule D (Form 1041)) or the 2003 Schedule D Tax Worksheet, see the instructions before completing this part.*

27 Enter the amount from Form 8801, line 10 27

28 Enter the amount from line 26 of your 2003 Schedule D (Form 1040) (line 23 of the 2003 Schedule D (Form 1041)) or line 13 of your 2003 Schedule D Tax Worksheet* 28

29 Enter the amount from line 19 of your 2003 Schedule D (Form 1040), or line 15d, column (2), of the 2003 Schedule D (Form 1041) . . . 29

30 If you did not complete the 2003 Schedule D Tax Worksheet, enter the amount from line 28. Otherwise, add lines 28 and 29, and enter the **smaller** of that result or the amount from line 10 of your 2003 Schedule D Tax Worksheet 30

31 Enter the **smaller** of line 27 or line 30 31

32 Subtract line 31 from line 27 32

33 If line 32 is $175,000 or less ($87,500 or less if married filing separately for 2003), multiply line 32 by 26% (.26). Otherwise, multiply line 32 by 28% (.28) and subtract $3,500 ($1,750 if married filing separately for 2003) from the result . . . . ▶ 33

34 Enter the amount from line 30 of your 2003 Schedule D (Form 1040) (line 27 of the 2003 Schedule D (Form 1041)) or line 19 of your Schedule D Tax Worksheet.* Enter -0- if you did not complete Part IV of your 2003 Schedule D (Form 1040) (Part V of 2003 Schedule D (Form 1041)) 34

35 Enter the **smaller** of line 27 or line 28 35

36 Enter the **smaller** of line 34 or line 35 36

37 If you did not complete a 2003 Schedule D Tax Worksheet for the regular tax or the AMT, enter the amount from your 2003 Schedule D (Form 1040), line 43 (or 2003 Schedule D (Form 1041), line 40) (or if that line is blank, the amount from your 2003 Schedule D (Form 1040), line 31 (or 2003 Schedule D (Form 1041), line 28)). Otherwise, enter the amount from line 32 of the Schedule D Tax Worksheet* (or if that line is blank, the amount from line 20 of that worksheet). 37

38 Enter the **smaller** of line 36 or line 37. If line 36 is zero, go to line 46 38

39 Multiply line 38 by 5% (.05) . . . . . . ▶ 39

40 Subtract line 38 from line 36. If zero or less, enter -0- and go to line 46 40

41 Enter your qualified 5-year gain, if any, from your 2003 Schedule D (Form 1040), line 35 (2003 Schedule D (Form 1041), line 32) . . 41

42 Enter the **smaller** of line 40 or line 41 42

43 Multiply line 42 by 8% (.08). . . . . . ▶ 43

44 Subtract line 42 from line 40 44

45 Multiply line 44 by 10% (.10) . . . . ▶ 45

46 Subtract line 38 from line 37 46

47 Subtract line 36 from line 35 47

48 Enter the **smaller** of line 46 or line 47 48

49 Multiply line 48 by 15% (.15) . . . . ▶ 49

50 Subtract line 48 from line 47 50

51 Multiply line 50 by 20% (.20) . . . . ▶ 51

If line 29 is zero or blank, skip lines 52 and 53 and go to line 54. Otherwise, go to line 52.

52 Subtract line 35 from line 31 52

53 Multiply line 52 by 25% (.25) . . . . ▶ 53

54 Add lines 33, 39, 43, 45, 49, 51, and 53 54

55 If line 27 is $175,000 or less ($87,500 or less if married filing separately), multiply line 27 by 26% (.26). Otherwise, multiply line 27 by 28% (.28) and subtract $3,500 ($1,750 if married filing separately) from the result 55

56 Enter the **smaller** of line 54 or line 55 here and on line 11 56

* The 2003 Schedule D Tax Worksheet is on page D-11 of the 2003 Instructions for Schedule D (Form 1040) (page 37 of the 2003 Instructions for Form 1041).

Form **8801** (2004)

chapter six:
AMT Planning

There is an old adage that says, "Those who fail to plan, plan to fail." How true it is! Will planning solve all the problems one faces? Of course not. But planning recognizes change and incorporates it into a process. While planning will not eliminate the perceived risk, it will reduce the consequential harm.

Tax Planning

Every problem has a solution. Granted, you may not like the solution, but there is a remedy. And the nature of that remedy depends largely on your perspective.

So it is with tax planning. Choices are made based upon one's perspective. For instance, the tax law gives certain *exemptions* from gross income. An individual taxpayer can choose to use this feature of the tax law to reduce, or in some cases, eliminate, his or her taxes.

Good tax planning is something you want. Bad tax planning is something you want to avoid. Common sense?

You bet, except that it is not always easy to spot. Any tax planning should be tested against the following points to be certain, from your unique individual perspective, that it is good tax planning.

- *Overly complex planning to get a tax benefit is many times bad planning.* Setting up offshore trusts (some call these AMT trusts to avoid the AMT) is so complex that it does not pass a common sense smell test. If it looks too good to be true, chances are it is. Good tax planning is not overly complex. While it may seem involved, you should be capable of understanding its basics. If not, watch out, because such planning is always subject to IRS attack.
- *Personal needs trump tax planning.* Good tax planning always begins with your needs. Getting a handle on the big picture is crucial. Ask yourself, *will this AMT plan meet my needs and goals? Will it cause me to be subject to an IRS audit? How will it affect my family or loved ones?*
- *Good tax planning is always ethical.* How do you know it is ethical? If the AMT plan is one that could be disclosed to the IRS or any other third party without recrimination, then it is probably ethical. Such ethical plans, by definition, are compliant with the tax law.
- *Avoid borderline tax plans.* These are AMT plans, for instance, that cannot be upheld on IRS audit or in court. If the AMT plan *more likely than not* results in negligence or similar penalties, it should

be avoided. If an AMT plan sounds borderline, have it reviewed by a second, independent tax advisor (and maybe even a third to break a tie).

- *Good tax planning always involves follow-up.* A good tax plan is one that works in execution as well as on paper. So telling an individual taxpayer to reduce TPIs (see Chapter 4) is practically irrelevant if the plan to actually reduce them is never implemented. And what is good tax planning today can become bad tax planning when implemented tomorrow because of a change in the tax law. Vigilance is the key.
- *Learn the jargon.* Know that the CPA or tax lawyer, like the doctor or banker, have their own jargon. Become familiar with the talk. That way, whenever you hear or read something relevant to your family's tax situation, you do not have to contact a costly professional.

The Internal Revenue Service

Understanding IRS jargon and the sources of information it provides will assist in your tax planning acumen. There are twelve major research sources used by tax planners that originate from Congress and the IRS. Other sources, such as court cases, can be consulted, but much of the language of tax planning is from the IRS.

1. Tax Law

Given by Congress, the most recent statutory tax law in the U.S. is the *1986 Internal Revenue Code*. This is where it all begins. Often, additional pieces of tax legislation are passed (like the 2001, 2002, and 2003 Tax Acts) that amend and make changes to the Code.

2. IRS Regulations

When the 16th Amendment to the Constitution created the federal income tax law, Congress designated the Internal Revenue Service as the administrative agency to manage the federal tax law (now the 1986 Internal Revenue Code).

To that end, the IRS has an executive, judicial, and legislative function (as do most government agencies). Its executive function is to enforce the tax law via collection actions and criminal and civil sanctions. The judicial function is a hearings process, commonly referred to as *audit*. The legislative function is the drafting and implementing of regulations.

Regulations issued by the IRS are either interpretative (over 90%) or legislative (perhaps 5%). An interpretative regulation *interprets* the tax law, while a legislative one acts as an additional tax law. Regulations also are issued as *proposed* (suggestions by IRS asking for comment), *temporary* (issued as proposed regulations and expire three years after issue), and *final* (must be followed as tax law).

While temporary and final regulations must be followed, temporary regulations are issued as proposed regulations, meaning that while all temporary regulations are proposed regulations, not all proposed regulations need be temporary regulations. Why is this important? Because proposed regulations modify nothing, but ask for mere suggestions. Proposed regulations that are not temporary need not be followed. However, in tax planning, such proposed regulations are an indication of the thinking of the IRS and should be carefully reviewed.

Note: *All income tax regulations have the number "1" directly before the Internal Revenue Code section that discusses that part of the income tax. So if the AMT section is 56, then 1.56 is the IRS regulation interpreting section 56.*

3. Revenue Rulings and Revenue Procedures

Revenue Rulings are an official interpretation of the tax law by the IRS and its conclusions are limited to the facts within it. Anyone can rely on it, and it is designated by the letters *Rev. Rul.* You can find Revenue Rulings in the *Cumulative Bulletin*, a collection of documents that can be purchased from the IRS. Many can be downloaded from the IRS website, **www.irs.gov**. Revenue Rulings are referenced, for example, like the following: Rev. Rul. 70-40, 1970-1 CB 50. It is the fortieth revenue ruling issued in 1970, found at the first volume of the Cumulative Bulletin on page 50.

While Revenue Rulings deal with the substance of tax law, *Revenue Procedures* focus on practice and procedure questions, such as how to compute depreciation and when to file a tax form. Revenue Procedures can be found the same way as you find Revenue Rulings, only substituting *Rev. Proc.* for Rev. Rul. in the citation.

4. Announcement or Notice

Issued by the IRS to address a broad area of the tax law, an Announcement or Notice has the same value as Revenue Rulings and Revenue Procedures.

5. News or Information Release

A news or information release is a press release, and carries little or no value. It is usually followed up with some sort of other IRS document, like a Revenue Ruling, Revenue Procedure, or Notice.

6. General Counsel Memorandum

A General Counsel Memorandum is a legal memo proposed by the IRS legal department, called the Office of Chief Counsel, and responds to the IRS personnel's request on technical tax law matters. (These are no longer issued by the IRS, but ones previously issued may still be relevant.)

7. Action on Decision

It is the policy of the Internal Revenue Service to announce at an early date whether it will follow the holdings in certain cases. An *Action on Decision* is the document making such an announcement. An Action on Decision will be issued at the discretion of the Service only on unappealed issues decided adverse to the government. Unlike a Treasury Regulation or a Revenue Ruling, an Action on Decision is not an affirmative statement of Service position. It is not intended to serve as public guidance and may not be cited as precedent.

In the Action on Decision, the IRS may acquiesce or nonacquiesce in the court's holdings. The recommendation will be summarized as acquiescence, acquiescence in result only, or nonacquiescence. Both *acquiescence* and *acquiescence in result only* mean that the IRS accepts the holding of the court in a case and that the IRS will follow it in disposing of cases with the same controlling facts. *Nonacquiescence* signifies that, although no further appeal will be sought, the IRS does not agree with the holding of the court. In those cases, it generally will not follow the decision in disposing of cases involving other taxpayers.

8. Private Letter Ruling

Taxpayers can write to the IRS national office (at 1111 Constitution Avenue in Washington, D.C.) and ask the IRS its opinion on a particular tax transaction. The IRS can respond with a *Private Letter Ruling*. For tax planning, these are vital. Once the IRS responds and the taxpayer follows its response, the IRS is bound by its opinion (generally preventing a future audit problem).

However, what is important about a Private Letter Ruling is that only the taxpayer who requested the ruling can rely upon it. Others could expect a similar response to a similar question, but there is no guarantee you would get the same response, and you get no protection for your actions from someone else's Private Letter Ruling.

9. Technical Advice Memorandum

Technical requests from an IRS district or appeals office are answered by the national office in memo form. *Technical Advice Memoranda* (TAM) are very helpful for planning.

10. Internal Revenue Manual

The Internal Revenue Manual is the tax bible for the IRS. It contains all the IRS policies, procedures, organization, etc. While not legally binding, it shows how the IRS views tax transactions, and most importantly, how it audits taxpayers. You can find it on the IRS website, **www.irs.gov**.

11. Auditor Guides

The IRS has issued, to its revenue agents and auditors, special IRS Audit Guides for specific types of taxpayers. Invaluable if the taxpayer is in the same industry (*e.g.*, used car dealers), but not legally binding.

12. Other IRS Documents and Publications

In addition to the document previously listed, the IRS produces hundreds of other documents and publications that can provide guidance and assist a taxpayer in his or her AMT planning. Some of these documents include the following:

- *Chief Counsel Advice Memoranda.* Written to IRS personnel, and are also called Service Center Advice, IRS Technical Assistance, IRS Legal Memorandum, and so on.

- *Field Service Advice Memoranda.* Similar to the Chief Counsel Advice Memoranda, except it covers a specific taxpayer in the field.
- *Publications.* Issued as general IRS literature, they provide public guidance.

AMT Planning Specifics

Armed with these ideas about good tax planning and IRS research sources, it is now time to consider specific AMT planning strategies. There are some general planning ideas you should practice every tax filing season related to the AMT.

- *AMT Exemption.* Your focus should be on the AMT exemption. In terms of the exemption (Chapter 1), do not forget that it looks like this:

Year	Married Filing Single	Married Filing Jointly	Single
2004-05	$40,250	$58,000	$29,000
2006 and future years	$33,750	$45,000	$22,500

- *Exclusions.* Another key idea for most individual taxpayers is that it is the exclusion items (Chapter 4, specifically) that require an AMT. Shifting income into a year when the AMT is already due can have significant savings.

Example:

Joan, a single individual, has been informed that she will receive a year-end bonus of $100,000 in January, 2006. If she does nothing, the incremental difference between her AMT exemption in 2006 versus 2005 is $6,500. So she will sacrifice an additional $6,500 of AMT exemption by receiving the bonus in 2006. She should request that it be paid in 2005.

- *Accelerating Income.* Means of accelerating income for an AMT year include shifting ordinary income (or capital gains) and redeeming CDs, treasury bills, and other fixed income maturity investments before year's end.
- *Passive Income and Losses.* Since passive losses are not deductible for the AMT, it is wise to increase the passive income (see Chapter 3) to offset the passive losses. The AMT will not be increased by such additional passive income.
- *Defer Nondeductible AMT Deductions.* Deferring nondeductible AMT deductions into future years can act for that future year in the same manner as shifting income from that year. For instance, the payment of real property taxes in 2005, attributable to 2004, is one such possibility. Obtaining a home equity mortgage for educational purposes and deferring the interest payment until 2005 is another example.
- *Crossover Point.* Always know your *crossover point.* This is where the tentative minimum tax

equals the regular tax and no AMT liability arises. It is the *load up* point in which the maximum number of adjustments and TPIs can be loaded into AMTI *without* triggering an AMT.

Example:

Chris has taxable income of $200,000 in 2003, which results in a regular tax of $70,000 (.35 x $200,000). His AMTI is $265,000, including $65,000 of AMT adjustments and TPIs, and produces a tentative minimum tax of about $70,000 ((.26 x $175,000) + (.28 x $90,000)). He is at the crossover point where the tentative minimum tax equals the regular tax. He can now decide whether to pay the AMT and generate an MTC for future years—or pay the regular tax.

How do you make the above crossover point determination? How do you decide to accelerate or defer income, accelerate or defer deductions, etc.? The answer is tax software.

- *Tax Software.* There are many good tax software packages available and some have an AMT planner. For example, see the industry leader, **www.turbotax.com**. Use the tax planning software especially in the fourth quarter of the year. Make projections and observe how the shifting of income and AMT nondeductible exclusion items can reduce the AMT liability. If you paid an AMT in a prior year, consider how the MTC can reduce your regular tax in this year (assuming no AMT is due).

Note: *Never overlook the abundant free IRS resources on its website. Always get Publication 17, Your Federal Income Taxes (Individuals) each year and note the new tax changes and how they may affect you and your family.*

If the software and your projections indicate a potential tax liability in the fourth quarter, consider readjusting your exemptions claimed on the W-4 filed with your employer. Request (which is your right) a new W-4 and adjust the exemption accordingly. (Remember, the greater the number of exemptions claimed, the less tax is taken from your pay. Conversely, the fewer exemptions claimed, the more tax is taken from your pay.)

If self-employed, readjust the last quarter estimated tax payment, keeping in mind any additional expenses on Schedule C, *Sole Proprietorship*, which would be deductible for AMT purposes. The trick is to break even (within $100) as an employee or self-employed.

Note: *The most sound financial planning results in a situation in which you do not pay Uncle Sam and you do not collect a refund. Why? Because the IRS pays no interest on your* *refund. Since money has a time value, inflation lets the IRS refund cheaper dollars to you than you originally paid over the past year.*

- *Tax Credits.* Focus on any tax credits (although in 2004, only three are permissible against the tentative minimum tax, along with the FTC) and possible carryovers.
- *Capital Gains.* Generally, income is classified as either *ordinary income* or *capital gains*. An easy way to remember the difference is that ordinary income is any income you receive from the sweat of your brow, such as wages, commissions, bonuses, salary, etc. Capital gains is income you receive that is *not* from the sweat of your brow, such as interest, rent, dividends, etc. (Ordinary income is taxed at a top tax rate of 35% (AMT rates are slightly lower—26% and 28%), and capital gains income is taxed (until the end of 2008) at only 15%.)

So, if at all possible, identify whether the source of the income to be paid is from ordinary sources or capital asset sources. A *capital asset* (sales or exchanges of stock, bond, investment real estate, etc.) that is held by you for more than twelve months will usually *avoid* the AMT rates of 26% and 28%, and be taxed at only 15%. This means that whenever you can convert an ordinary asset into capital gains, you should legally try to do so. This can be accomplished quite simply.

Every gain or loss when property is disposed of is treated as either ordinary or capital. To have a capital gain or loss, you need a capital asset. Capital assets must be from a sale (cash for property) or an exchange (property for property) *and* meet the tax definition of a capital asset. This tax definition states that *every* asset or property item is a capital asset unless it falls within one of the following eight exceptions:

1. inventory or property held for sale to customers;
2. accounts or notes receivable (customer or client IOUs);
3. supplies used in a business;
4. real estate (raw land), depreciable real estate (rental property), tangible personal property (machinery), and intangible property subject to periodic write-off or amortization;
5. intellectual property (copyrights, literary, musical or artistic compositions, etc.) held by its creator or a person to whom the property was gifted by the creator (notice that this definition *excludes* patents);
6. certain U.S. government publications;
7. certain dealer-held commodity derivative financial investments; and,
8. hedging transactions.

If the property falls in any one of the eight exceptions, it is automatically an ordinary income item, triggering a possible tax rate of 35% and an AMT rate. If not, it is a capital gains or loss item, producing the lower 15% tax rate and *no* AMT.

You can convert ordinary income into capital gains by holding the property for more than twelve months. So with a little planning, it is quite easy to convert ordinary income from a capital asset held for twelve months or less and taxed up to 35%, to capital gains and taxed up to only 15%.

Example:

Tony owns stock in IBM Corporation (a capital asset) that he sells after holding the stock for exactly twelve months. His gain is subject to the AMT and can be taxed up to 35% as ordinary income. Had he held the stock for just one more day, he would be able to legally convert the ordinary income from a short-term (twelve months or less) capital asset to capital gains from a long-term (more than twelve months) capital asset.

Note: *It is possible to pay an AMT in a year with large long-term capital gains. If your long-term capital gains are enough to cause the AMTI to wipe out the AMT exemption (e.g., $40,250 if your AMTI is less than $112,500), the AMT rates can apply.*

To avoid this result, time your long-term capital gains—do not take all the gains in one year; spread them out over several years; or match them against capital losses.

- *Review Income, Losses, and Credits.* While the tax software can help in this regard, the AMT generally ignores certain interest, business losses, and foreign tax credits. (see Chapter 5.)

Note: *If you receive income from judgments or settlements in an employment contract dispute or personal injury case (e.g., auto accident), there is a substantial problem with the deduction for attorney fees. For instance, a taxpayer with a $500,000 judgment that includes a $200,000 attorney fee (40% contingent attorney fee), can deduct the $200,000 as a miscellaneous deduction for regular tax purposes. However, none of the $200,000 is allowed for AMT purposes.*

Example:

Mr. Alexander settled an employment contract dispute with his employer for $250,000, of which $245,100 represented legal fees (he also received an additional $100,000 on an age discrimination claim). While the legal fees were deductible as a miscellaneous itemized deduction, subject to the 2% floor, for regular tax purposes, the tax court found no such deduction available under the AMT.

RESULT—The IRS was successful in obtaining an AMT of more than $57,000 on the disallowed legal fees of $245,100.

Alexander v. Commissioner, T.C. Memo 1995-51

Specific AMT Planning Tips

Aside from the general points discussed previously, consider the following specific AMT planning tips.

Taxable Income

The AMT computation begins with the taxable income from Form 1040. (see Chapter 1.) That figure, in turn, comes from the taxpayer's *gross income* for the year. So it makes sense to recognize the basic components of that income.

The two basic components of gross income are *ordinary income* (salary, wages, commissions, profits from business, etc.) and *capital gains income* (gains from the sale or exchange of capital assets, like stocks or bonds). Ordinary income and short-term capital gains (capital assets held for twelve months or less) can be taxed up to 35%, but long-term capital gains (capital assets held for more than twelve months)—for both regular tax and the AMT—are generally taxed at only 15%.

An earlier planning tip suggested that converting ordinary income into capital gains by holding capital assets for more than twelve months before sale is a wise planning maneuver. However, do not confuse conversion of ordinary income to capital gains with additional capital gain income.

Example:

Mr. and Mrs. Payne are California residents and have taxable income in 2004 of $200,000 and no long-term capital gains. They lose part of the AMT exemption of $58,000 because their taxable income exceeds $150,000. (Recall from Chapter 1 that the AMT exemption phases out in $0.25 increments for every $1 married taxpayers earn over $150,000. At $150,000, taxpayers receive the full $58,000 exemption, but at $382,000, they receive nothing.) The Paynes still have an AMT exemption of $45,500

$200,000 - $150,000 = $50,000 x .25 = $12,500;
$58,000 - $12,500 = $45,500

or an AMT liability of about $40,000.

$200,000 - $45,500 = $154,500 x .26 = $40,170

Note: *The AMT denies any deduction for state, local, or property taxes, and for 2004-2005, any state sales taxes. In high tax states, like California, there is no AMT deduction for state capital gains taxes (up to 9.3% in California) for AMT purposes. That means the 20% effective capital gains rate for the Paynes, as California residents, is even higher.*

Planning Tip

The timing of your capital gains income is critical to the AMT computation. Had the Paynes converted some of their ordinary income into long-term capital gains, then a portion of the AMT exemption would be available and the California capital gains tax would be less. The result would be a lower AMT and lower overall effective capital gains tax.

Expenses

Expenses for individual taxpayers are generally those cash disbursements that result in deductible or nondeductible items on a tax return. For instance, expenses for personal items (groceries, clothes, etc.) are not deductible for either regular tax or AMT purposes.

Note: *Unlike accelerating income into an AMT year, expenses need to be delayed or deferred into a regular tax year when they will be deductible, since many legitimate expenses are not deductible for AMT purposes. Also, deferring charitable expense deductions to a regular tax year means that the effective cost of the deduction is less because the marginal tax rate for regular tax (35%) exceeds the top marginal rate for the AMT (28%).*

Many legitimate expenses (for example, unreimbursed employee expenses) are deductible for regular tax purposes. Such expenses for the AMT are not. As discussed in Chapter 2, miscellaneous deductions are generally disallowed for the AMT.

The AMT does allow, however, all Schedule C (sole proprietorship) expenses. So a nondeductible (Schedule A) itemized expense becomes a fully deductible (Schedule C) expense. For instance, a nondeductible tax expense might be attributable to business use of the home and be partially tax deductible.

Planning Tip

Convert as many Schedule A (itemized deductions) expenses that are disallowed for AMT purposes or limited for regular tax purposes as possible to Schedule C (sole proprietorship) expenses. How? Understand the purpose of Schedule C. It is designed to reflect an individual taxpayer's independent contractor status. In short, working not as an employee, partner, or shareholder, but as a sole practitioner or proprietor.

Example:

Betty, a single mother of two, is concerned about the AMT. She has done her AMT projections and believes it will be a problem. So Betty creates a legitimate side business—managing neighborhood garage sales for communities as a consultant. She reports expenses that were itemized as business expenses (tax preparation, newspapers and garage sale periodicals, taxes, etc.), which not only reduce her ordinary income from the business, but become AMT deductible.

Note: *Obviously, not all miscellaneous deductions can be recharacterized as Schedule C expenses. Timing, once again, controls. Pay such expense deductions in a year when the regular tax applies, not the AMT.*

Consider Your Total Tax Liability

This means keep your eye on your *total* tax liability. Never just focus entirely on one tax year.

Planning Tip

It is crucial to remember that the AMT in one year produces an MTC for use against regular tax in a later year. Consequently, there are many situations in which paying an AMT in one year or very soon will reduce total taxes paid. Conversely, it is possible to accelerate income into an AMT year or defer non-AMT deductions and reduce AMT liability, but increase total tax liability between the two years.

Example:

In doing his AMT projections for 2004, David has taxable income of $200,000, for a regular tax of $70,000 (.35 x $200,000).

His AMTI is $265,000, including $65,000 of adjustments and TPIs, for an AMT of approximately $70,000 (.26 x $175,000 + .28 x $90,000).

He is at the *crossover point* where the tentative minimum tax equals the regular tax.

He now decides to increase an adjustment item of real estate tax in 2004 that will result in an additional $10,000 deduction for regular tax, but only an $8,000 adjustment for AMT purposes. His *new* taxable income is $190,000 with a regular tax liability of $66,500 (.35 x $190,000).

His AMTI is now $273,000, including $73,000 of adjustments (up from $65,000) for a tentative minimum tax of $72,940 ((.26 x $175,000) + (.28 x 98,000)), or an AMT of $6,440.

When the dust settles, David reduced his 2004 total tax liability. This tax savings of $560 (.28 x $2000[$10,000 - $8000]) results from paying the AMT in 2004. In addition, the

MTC of $6,440 may be carried forward to succeeding years to offset regular tax liability when the above adjustment reverses in future years.

In the previous example, the acceleration of adjustments into an AMT year resulted in a greater AMT, but lower *overall* taxes. However, you must be cautious of accelerating income to increase your regular tax liability over your AMT liability. If you increase your tax rate to the 35% level and lose your MTC due to no AMT being paid, you may actually increase your total tax liability.

Example:
In 2004, Morgan decides to accelerate income into an AMT year based on financial projections, thereby increasing her regular tax liability and reducing her AMT liability. While the AMT is avoided, the increase in Morgan's marginal rate to 35% from the AMT level of 28% on the incremental income causes her to pay more total tax in 2004. Plus, there is now no MTC that can be used against the regular tax in future years.

Adjustments

Of the thirteen adjustments covered in Chapters 2 and 3, only those primarily from Chapter 2 are most likely adjustments for individual taxpayers, and will be the focus of AMT tax planning.

Incentive Stock Options

As you may recall from Chapter 2, there is no regular tax upon the exercise of an incentive stock option. Only when the shares are sold is there an impact on the regular tax—and then it is capital gains. But the AMT is not as nice. You may pay an AMT upon exercise (even though not one share of stock is sold). Such a result can be disastrous in a declining market.

Planning Tip

If you have incentive stock options about to lapse, do one of the following.

- Exercise and sell the stock in the same year. This is the easiest route and results in the total avoidance of the AMT.
- Exercise and do not sell in the same year provided no AMT is due despite the AMT adjustment (because other adjustments are negative, regular taxable income is greater than AMTI, size of the option does not put you over the AMT exemption, etc.).

Example:

Rick had to exercise his ISOs or they would lapse. He exercised in 1999 and paid an AMT of $75,000 by borrowing the proceeds. He believed that he could recoup this amount when he sold the stock. Unfortunately, the bear market struck and Rick sold the stock at a loss.

While he could use the capital loss to offset any capital gains plus $3,000 of ordinary income per year for tax purposes and carryover the excess capital losses to date of death, he has had to pay $75,000 in AMT. Some relief may be had, if in future years, he has no AMT liability and can use the minimum tax credit to offset his regular tax. However, this credit will have an inflation-discounted future basis, making its value decrease the longer he must wait before being able to use it.

Planning Tip

It may not be wise to avoid the AMT if *total* tax liability is increased. The exercise of ISOs must be carefully reviewed *before* the date of exercise arises. Many of the excellent software programs, Quicken, Turbotax, etc. will assist you in making this decision. Plus, never overlook the fact that you need the cash to do it.

There is also the possibility of making a regular tax election, known as an 83(b) tax election, that includes the current fair market value of the stock into gross income when the option is granted. Ordinarily, this election is made to qualify any future price appreciation as capital gain versus ordinary income, and such appreciation is deferred until the sale or exchange of the stock. Such an election reduces the AMTI in the eventual year of exercise. But caution is warranted because if the stock does *not* appreciate, you will have paid the regular tax (and reduced the AMT) for nothing—since you will not exercise a stock option that has a market value of stock below its option price.

Example:

Mr. and Mrs. Miller pay $100,000 to exercise Mr. Miller's ISOs. They believe that the stock will appreciate and a timely profit will be made. They finance the exercise with a second mortgage on their home.

Unfortunately, the stock declines in value and they are faced with a $100,000 debt and an AMT liability in the year of exercise. To make matters worse, the interest on the home equity loan is not deductible for AMT purposes, since the loan proceeds were not used to acquire, construct, or improve a residence.

Note: *If you may be in a similar circumstance as the previous example, ask your employer for stock appreciation rights (SARS) or some other stock award program that can be liquidated to provide the needed cash to exercise any future ISOs. (Loans to officers for purposes of exercising ISOs are no longer permitted in public companies because of the Sarbanes-Oxley Act of 2002, and are frowned upon in many private enterprises as well.)*

An easy way to decide the number of ISOs to exercise and still avoid the AMT is as follows.

1. Compute the regular tax (Form 1040).
2. Compute the AMT (Form 6251).
3. Subtract step 1 from step 2.
4. Divide step 3 by 26% (the AMT rate).
5. Divide step 4 by the spread per share. The quotient is the maximum number of ISO shares that may be exercised without AMT.

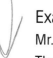

Example:

James, a single taxpayer, has multiple ISOs to exercise as VP of sales. His regular tax is $20,000 and AMT is $15,000. The $5,000 difference divided by the 26% AMT rate is $19,320. Assuming that the spread per share is $20, the maximum number of shares James can exercise without incurring an AMT is 966 shares.

Interest

As noted in Chapter 2, only qualified housing interest is deductible for AMT purposes. That is, interest on a loan is generally deductible for AMT purposes if the loan proceeds are used to acquire, construct, or substantially improve the residence. If it is a refinancing, the amount cannot exceed the debt outstanding immediately before the refinancing.

Note: *Qualified housing interest naturally comes from a qualified residence. This is the taxpayer's principal residence and one other secondary property selected by the taxpayer and used as his or her residence. Such residence is any qualified dwelling—house, apartment, cooperative, condominium, or permanent mobile home. Houseboats can qualify only as a primary but never secondary residence for AMT purposes.*

Planning Tip

Borrowed home equity funds can only be used to acquire, construct, or improve a residence and be deductible for AMT purposes. Be certain that such loans are used for this purpose.

Example 1:

Jeff borrows money using a home equity loan, the proceeds of which will be used for credit card liquidation and his child's education. AMT gives no interest deduction for this long-term loan, which will impact several years.

Example 2:

Dad borrows against his home equity and uses the proceeds for a down payment on his recently married son's residence. Unless Dad can show that this is a second residence (unlikely, considering it is either a personal loan to the son or an outright gift), the AMT gives no deduction.

Example 3:

Todd resides in Michigan and maintains another residence in Naples, Florida. He used the Naples residence to secure a loan, the proceeds of which were used to purchase a condominium in New Orleans. He then used the equity in the New Orleans condominium to purchase a yacht. For regular tax purposes, the interest qualifies as deductible because it does not have the same restriction of the interest deduction on *home* indebtedness as the AMT.

For regular tax purposes, the latter loan is deductible for regular tax and should be used in years when no AMT is due. Conversely, the taxpayer will want to use the interest on the Naples residence in AMT years, since it is deductible for regular tax and the AMT.

Medical Expenses

As you may recall, a deduction for medical expenses has a higher threshold floor for AMT purposes—10% versus 7.5% of AGI for regular tax. This results in a 2.5% of AGI increment.

Planning Tip

- Eliminate all AMT on medical expenses. Participate in an employer tax advantaged health savings plan. This virtually eliminates the deduction for regular tax and AMT purposes while allowing you to reduce your taxable income.
- Consider bunching medical expenses. Over various taxable years, bunch medical expenses with the purpose of exceeding the 10% of AGI floor.

Example:

In 2003, Michele prepays unreimbursed medical expenses for a medical procedure to be performed in early 2004. This creates an excess itemized deduction over the 10% of AGI limit, and such expenses are then deductible for AMT purposes.

Planning Tip

- Shift the medical expenses to a regular tax year. When bunching medical expenses together to reach the 10% of AIG floor for AMT purposes, consider shifting such unreimbursed expenses to a regular tax year with the lower 7.5% of AGI floor. It is an easy matter to shift medical expenses to a regular tax year by delaying payment or having an elective medical procedure (e.g., cosmetic surgery) performed and paid in a regular tax year.

Miscellaneous Deduction

Certain miscellaneous deductions are deductible for both regular tax and the AMT. The ones that are not are the ones that qualify for the 2% of AGI floor. Those are only deductible for regular tax purposes.

> **Planning Tip**
>
> - Convert the miscellaneous 2% itemized deductions that are not AMT deductible on Schedule A to trade or business expense deductions on Schedule C.
> - Legal fees for contract disputes, personal injury judgments, settlements, etc. are taxable income, but not allowed as an AMT deduction. The deduction for such fees are miscellaneous itemized deductions subject to the 2% floor. Consider treating such legal fees as trade or business deductions on Schedule C.
> - If it is not possible to convert the miscellaneous deduction to trade or business expenses, then pay them in a regular tax year. This is done by deferring the 2% deductions to a regular tax year. Also, accelerate the non-2% deductions into the AMT year, particularly in years when taxpayer's income reduces or eliminates the AMT exemption.
> - If you incur expense in your job, ask your employer to not use a nonaccountable business expense plan. If it is nonaccountable (employer gives an expense advance check and employee retains no records) and the reimbursement is included in your gross income, no AMT deduction is allowed. (Plus, an accountable business expense plan benefits both employer and employee.)

Note: *The American Jobs Creation Act of 2004 allows an above the line deduction for attorney fees and costs stemming from unlawful discrimination cases. This means that* *for the regular tax, such amounts are deductible as a non-itemized deduction.*

Example 1:

Kurt will incur legitimate 2% miscellaneous expense deductions from a job search. He decides to schedule his search and attendant expenses (*e.g.*, résumé service) to next year because he will be subject to the regular tax.

Example 2:

Lynn has a salary of $200,000 with $40,000 of unreimbursed expenses, and owes about $45,000 in regular tax. If her employer pays $20,000 of unreimbursed expenses with a reduction of $20,000 in her salary, the employer reduces its payroll, workers' compensation costs, and other insurance costs. Lynn's salary is now $180,000, and with $20,000 in miscellaneous itemized deductions, her regular tax liability declines and an AMT deduction results.

AMT Basis and Depreciation

An asset's cost basis is not the same for regular tax and the AMT. For example, an asset costing $20,000 may be depreciated under the regular tax at $10,000 for an adjusted basis of $10,000, but under the AMT at $8,000 for an adjusted basis of $12,000. This *dual basis* can result in a different gain or loss for your regular tax liability versus your AMT liability.

Upon sale, the difference between the regular tax gain or loss and the AMT gain or loss is an AMT adjustment. So if the

AMT basis is greater than the regular tax basis, then a negative adjustment results (as is usually the case).

> **Planning Tip**
>
> Keep the AMT basis higher than the regular tax basis.

Taxes

No taxes are generally allowed for AMT purposes. However, the generation-skipping transfer tax and one-half of the self-employment tax are allowed for both regular tax and the AMT. Since the only benefit of most taxes is to lower the regular tax, bunch the taxes by prepaying into a regular tax year.

> **Planning Tip**
>
> Where possible and reasonable, convert taxes to trade and business expenses. For example, hold your principal residence in a limited liability partnership (LLP) or limited liability corporation (LLC). This allows the entity to own the property, pay the taxes, and take the requisite deductions on its return. Likewise, if you live in a state that imposes a personal (*ad valorem*) tax on such things as automobiles and boats, title these assets in a business name and deduct them for both regular tax and AMT purposes on Schedule C.

Standard Deduction

The AMT does not allow for the standard deduction. With this in mind, try to bunch itemized deductions in different years to exceed the standard deduction. This will lower your regular tax liability. If you can bunch itemized deductions that are fully allowed for both regular tax and the AMT—medical expenses in excess of 10% floor, qualified housing interest, casualty losses, charitable contributions, and non-2% miscellaneous deductions—you can lower both your regular tax and AMT liability.

Tax Preference Items

Of the five TPIs, only qualified private activity bonds (PABs), have any real flexibility in AMT planning for individuals. (Recall that a TPI, unlike an adjustment, can only increase AMTI.)

Every investor with tax-exempt bonds, whether in individual bonds or bond funds, needs to reevaluate these investments. Either the original bond registration statement or Form 1099 will identify the tax exempt as subject to the AMT.

Planning Tip

- Do a tax-free swap of one tax-exempt for another tax-exempt (the latter being a non-AMT bond). Recognize that your yield to maturity on the non-AMT bond will be less, but consider the lower AMT for all the years you hold that bond.
- Seek out AMT-free funds. Several major issuers (Touchstone, Fidelity, T. Rowe Price, etc.) offer such funds, and all have websites.
- Retain the AMT-PAB bonds with the higher yields, provided you are in a regular tax year.

Note: *The Comprehensive AMT Problems at the end of this chapter shows what can happen if you misjudge and have a PAB in an AMT year.*

MTC

A final consideration for AMT planning is the use of the minimum tax credit (MTC). The goal is to obtain an MTC in an AMT year to be used in later years when a regular tax is due. To accomplish this, you must avoid adjustments that do not produce an MTC. These adjustments, known as *exclusion preferences*, should be shifted to a regular tax year.

Example:

Brian has refinanced his home and used the proceeds for his child's education. This interest is an exclusion preference that is nondeductible for AMT purposes. It should be used in a regular tax year, rather than an AMT year. If next year is an AMT year, then Brian should take this deduction in the current year for regular tax purposes.

Planning Tip

Since the selling of shares of stock obtained through an ISO can actually increase your MTC, make sure that anytime you exercise an ISO that results in an AMT liability, every subsequent tax year file both Form 6251 and Form 8801 until the MTC is claimed.

Note: *The value of the MTC is questionable if a taxpayer is constantly subject to the AMT—an increasing number of taxpayers are entering this category. (see Chapter 1.) If this* *is the case, then the preceding example makes little sense for a taxpayer, because year two would be an AMT year as well. The Comprehensive AMT Problems that follow shows how the MTC is computed and carried forward.*

130

The Ten Things to Watch that ca[n] Make or Break you AMT

1. **Credits.** The more credits you claim the more likely you will pay the AMT. Watch this area.

2. **ISOs.** Do not exercise large ISOs unless you want to pay an AMT.

3. **Interest on Second Mortgages.** Watch how the proceeds of second mortgages are used. It is okay if used for buying, building, or improving a residence, but not for other purposes like financing a college education.

4. **Long-Term Capital Gains.** Converting ordinary income into capital gains can avoid the AMT, but be careful, as large long-term capital gains can wipe out the AMT exemption.

5. **Medical Expenses.** Since the amount of medical deductions is severely limited for the AMT versus the regular tax, consider matching these expenses with spreading over several years.

6. **Miscellaneous Itemized Deductions.** Watch the unreimbursed employee expenses, tax preparation fees, investment expenses, etc., which are not deductible for AMT purposes. Consider shifting these expenses to Schedule C if you can legitimately claim them as business expenses.

7. **Personal Exemptions.** Know that the more personal exemptions claimed, the greater the likelihood for an AMT liability.

8. **Standard Deduction.** There is no standard deduction for AMT purposes, so you may need to consider itemizing those deductions you can, as it may reduce your total tax liability, even if it raises your regular tax liability.

9. **State and Local Taxes.** For 2004 and 2005, state sales tax itemized deductions may be claimed in lieu of state income taxes. Regardless of the state or local taxes claimed, they will push you toward the AMT.

10. **Tax-exempt Interest.** Watch for PABs, which are nonqualified MUNIs and can trigger an AMT.

• • • • • •

The following is a capstone review of many of the areas discussed in this book. Try to carefully follow this example and see if you can identify the areas that are similar to your situation and look for ways your tax liability for AMT can be reduced. Also, review how the AMT credit carryforward is computed.

Comprehensive AMT Problems

Married Family with Three Children

Background Tax Information

Mr. and Mrs. Jones are typical middle-class taxpayers with three children trying to make ends meet. Mr. Jones, an engineer, and Mrs. Jones, a teacher, are both employed and have the following tax information for taxable year 2003.

Income

Salaries	$125,000
Dividends	$2,000
Interest income	$3,000
Passive rental income	$24,000
Rental expenses	<$32,900>
Net passive rental loss	<$8,900>
Net long-term capital gain	$5,000
Qualified private activity bond income	$1,000

Expenses

Moving expenses	$12,500
Penalty on early withdrawal of savings	$500
Unreimbursed medical expenses	$14,000
State and local income taxes	$10,800
Real estate taxes	$8,500
Personal property taxes	$1,500
Home mortgage interest	$7,000
Home equity interest *(to pay off credit cards)*	$3,500
Investment interest	$8,500
Personal interest *(credit cards)*	$1,000
Charitable contributions	$10,000
Theft loss *(jewelry)*	$15,000
Unreimbursed employee expenses	$3,000
Safe deposit box rental	$120
Publication subscriptions	$300
Creditable foreign taxes from international mutual fund	$500
Pre-1987 accelerated depreciation	$10,000

Regular Tax Computation (Form 1040)

Mr. and Mrs. Jones' status is married filing jointly in 2003, with five personal exemptions.

Gross Income

Salaries	$125,000
Dividends	$2,000
Interest income	$3,000
Net LTG	$5,000

Net passive rental loss		<$8,900>
Qualified private activity bond income*		-0-
(tax-exempt)		
Gross income before adjustments		$126,100
Deductible adjustments:		
Moving expenses	<$12,500>	
Penalty on early withdrawal of savings	<$500>	
Total Adjustments		<$13,000>
Adjusted Gross Income (AGI)		$113,100

Itemized Deductions:

Unreimbursed medical expenses*		$5,518
**($14,000 - (.075 x $113,100))*		
State/local income tax	$10,800	
Real estate tax	$8,500	
Personal property tax	$1,500	
Total taxes paid		$20,800
Home mortgage interest	$7,000	
Home equity mtg. interest	$3,500	
Investment interest*	$5,000	
**($3,000 + $2,000—expense allowed to extent of income)*		
Personal interest	-0-	
Total interest paid		$15,500
Charitable contributions		$10,000
Theft loss*		$3,590
**($15,000 - $100 - (.10 x $113,100))*		

Miscellaneous Deductions:

Unreimbursed employee expenses	$3,000	
Safe deposit box rental	$120	
Publication subscriptions	$300	
Total Miscellaneous Deductions	$3,420	
Allowable miscellaneous deductions*		$1,158
**(3420 - (.02 x 113,100)*		
Total itemized deductions		<$56,566>
Taxable income before personal exemptions*		$56,534
**($113,100 - $56,566)*		
Personal exemptions *(5 x $3,050)*		<$15,250>
Taxable Income		$41,284
Regular Tax Before Credits *(tax tables)*		$5,491
Less: Foreign Tax Credit		<$500>
Net Regular Tax Liability before refundable credits		$4,991

AMT Calculation

Based on the Jones' initial estimates and software projections, they must consider the AMT.

AMT Computation (Form 6251)

Taxable Income before personal exemption	$56,534

Adjustments Total Taxable Income:		
Unreimbursed medical expenses*		$2,828
**(.025 x $113,100)*		
Taxes:		
State/local income tax	$10,800	
Real estate taxes	$8,500	
Personal property taxes	$1,500	
Total taxes paid		$20,800
Home equity mortgage interest		$3,500
(not used for acquisition or improvement)		
Miscellaneous deductions		$1,158
Passive activity losses		$8,900
Personal exemptions		$15,250
Total Adjustments		$52,436

Tax Preference items

Qualified private activity bond interest	$1,000	
Excess accelerated depreciation (Pre-1987)	$10,000	
Total Tax Preference Items		$11,000
AMTI		$119,970
AMT Exemption		<$58,000>
Net AMTI		$61,970
Tentative AMT *(.26 x $61,970)*		$16,112
Less: AMT Foreign Tax Credit		<$500>
Net Tentative AMT		$15,612
Less: Net Regular Tax		<$4,991>
AMT		$10,612

Based on the above, the Jones have a 2003 tax liability before refundable credits of $15,612, comprised of a regular tax of $4,991 and an AMT of $10,621. At this time, they should compute, using Form 8801, their Minimum Tax Credit (MTC) carryforward.

Minimum Tax Carryforward Computation (Form 8801)

Taxable Income (Form 6251)		$56,534
Adjustments to Taxable Income (Form 6251)		$52,436
Tax Preference Items:		
Qualified private activity bond interest	$1,000	
Excess accelerated depreciation (Pre-1987)*	-0-	

**The $10,000 TPI for accelerated depreciation is not included in the MTC because it is not a tax preference item for the MTC.*

Tax Preference Items for Credit	$1,000
AMTI For Credit	$109,970
AMT Exemption	<$58,000>
Net AMTI For Credit	$51,970
Tentative AMT For Credit*	$13,512
**(.26 x $51,970)*	
Net Regular Tax	<$4,991>
AMT For MTC	$8,521

AMT (2003)	$15,612
AMT for MTC	<$8,521>
MTC Carryforward (2004)	$7,091

Married with No Children

Background Tax Information

Mr. Caruso is married with no dependents and is the sole shareholder in an S corporation known as Caruso's Deli, Inc. During 2003, he sells his entire stock interest in the corporation for a taxable long-term capital gain of $1.0 million. Also, he had $100,000 in wages and $3,000 in charitable contributions (no other itemized deductions). His spouse was not employed in 2003. He also had interest from savings accounts (CDs) of $75,000.

Regular Tax Computation (Form 1040)

Mr. and Mrs. Caruso file a joint tax return in 2003.

Gross income:	
Wages	$100,000
Interest	$7,500
Schedule D *(Sale of Caruso Stock)*	$1,000,000
AGI	$1,107,500
Standard Deductions	<$9,500>
Personal Exemptions	<$6,100>
Taxable Income	$1,091,900
Ordinary income tax on $91,900	$16,601
Capital gains tax *(.15 x 1.0 million)*	$150,000
Regular tax liability *(tax tables)*	$166,601

AMT Calculation (Form 6251)

The sale of stock from the business requires Caruso to consider the AMT.

Taxable income		$1,091,900
Add Adjustments:		
Standard deduction	$9,500	
Personal exemptions	$6,100	
		$15,600
MTI		$1,107,500
AMT exemption*		-0-
**loss of full exemption because he exceeds income limitations*		
Net AMTI		$1,107,500
Ordinary income AMT *(.26 x $107,500)*		$27,950
Capital gain AMT *(.15 x $1.0 million)*		$150,000
TMT		$177,950
Less: Regular Tax Liability		<$166,601>
AMT		$11,349

Based on the above, Mr. Caruso has a 2003 tax liability before refundable credits of $177,950, comprised of a regular tax liability of $166,601 and an AMT liability of $11,349. Had Caruso financed the sale of his business by the use of an installment note and spread the $1.0 million gain over several years, he most likely would have avoided the AMT exposure.

Note: *Mr. Caruso had an S corporation. The American Jobs Creation Act of 2004 made major changes to all S corpo-*

rations. For instance, in the case of family S corporations, there is a new provision that treats all members of a family (spouse, children, etc.) as one S corporation shareholder. If you are the owner of an S corporation, consult with your accountant to determine how the changes in the law affect you.

Single with No Children

Background Tax Information

Ms. Darby, a bank officer in the commercial loan department, received a base salary of $80,000 and a commission of $20,000 in 2003. She is single with no dependents. In addition to salary and commissions, she has qualifying dividends of $3,500 and no other income. She owns a residence that she has borrowed $9,500 against to loan funds to her sister (for her medical school tuition). She also exercised an ISO on bank stock for $5,500 in 2003, but never sold the stock.

Regular Tax Computation (Form 1040)

Ms. Darby files as a single taxpayer in 2003:

Gross income:		
Wages		$100,000
Dividends		$3,500
AGI		$103,500
Less: Itemized deductions		
State, local, real estate taxes	$25,500	
Home equity loan interest *(used for personal purposes)*	$9,500	

Charitable contributions	$1,200	
Total itemized deductions		<$36,200>
Less: Personal exemption		<$3,050>
Taxable income		$64,250
Regular tax liability *(tax tables)*		$12,879

AMT Calculation (Form 6251)

Taxable income		$64,250
Add: Adjustments:		
State, local, real estate tax	$25,550	
Home equity loan interest	$9,500	
Personal exemption	$3,050	
		$38,050
AMTI		$102,300
Less: AMT exemption*		<$40,250>

**full exemption allowed. She does not exceed income limitation*

Net AMTI		$62,050
TMT *(.26 x $62,050)*		$16,133
Less: Regular tax liability		($12,879)
AMT		$3,254

Based on the calculations above, as a single taxpayer Mr. Darby has a 2003 tax liability before refundable credits of $16,133, comprised of a regular tax liability of $12,879 and an AMT liability of $3,254. Had she financed her sister's loan in some other manner (or spread it out over several years), she could have significantly avoided her AMT exposure.

Retired with Grown Children

Background Tax Information

Mr. and Mrs. Elder are retired, and their four sons have their own families and live apart from them. They are both age 72 and have excellent health. Their 2003 income consists of $7,000 in interest (CDs), $5,000 in dividends, taxable pension payments from their former employers of $15,000, taxable IRA distributions of $12,000, SSA-1099 Social Security payments of $20,000, and earnings from Mr. Elder's part-time teaching of $5,000. They contribute $1,500 to their church and have their medical expenses fully covered with insurance from Mrs. Elder's former employer. Their real estate taxes amount to $3,000 and they have no other taxes.

Regular Tax Computation (Form 1040)

Mr. and Mrs. Elder file a joint tax return in 2003:

Gross Income:		
Wages	$5,000	
Interest	$7,000	
Dividends	$5,000	
Pension Payments	$15,000	
IRA Distributions	$12,000	
Social Security Benefits*	$14,500	

**Because the Elders' taxable income $54,000 exceeds their 2003 base amount of $32,000 (MFJ), $14,500 of SSA-1099 benefits are taxable.*

AGI		$58,500

Standard Deduction*		<$11,400>
**The standard deduction in 2003 is increased from $9,500 to $11,400 for joint filers who are 65 or older.*		
Personal Exemptions		<$6,100>
Taxable Income		$41,000
Regular Tax Liability *(tax tables)*		$5,454

AMT Calculation (Form 6251)

Taxable income		$41,000
Add Adjustments:		
Standard Deductions	$11,400	
Personal Exemptions	$6,100	
		$17,500
AMTI		$58,500
Less: AMT Exemption*		<$58,000>
**full exemption allowed*		
Net AMTI		$500
TMT *(.26 x $500)*		$130
Less: Regular Tax Liability		<$5,454>
AMT		-0-

Based on the above, as is the usual case for most retirees, there is rarely an AMT due. But keep in mind that an AMT liability can arise if retirees itemize their deductions. Most retirees have few itemized deductions because they own their principal residence free and clear, but if there are unreimbursed medical deductions, the AMT adjustment for such deductions could create an AMT liability.

• • • • • •

Final Thoughts

You now have an understanding of the AMT. This understanding may be that it is beyond what you want to comprehend. Recall that in the preface that I indicated after finishing the book it is not likely (nor even recommended) that you complete Form 6251 for the AMT without any assistance. Follow that advice, but know that you have a better understanding of how you can work with your tax preparer to minimize and reduce your total tax liability.

Glossary

A

accelerated cost recovery system (ACRS). A method of depreciation that allows for rapid deduction of the cost of an asset. It was used for assets depreciated between 1981 and 1986. *See MACRS.*

accelerated depreciation. A method of depreciation that allows for faster write-off of the cost of property than straight-line depreciation. *See ACRS and MACRS.*

accrual method of accounting. A method of accounting that allows for income reported in the year it is earned and expenses reported in the year they are incurred.

adjusted basis. The computation necessary for determining a gain or loss on the sale or exchange of property. It begins with the cost of the property and increases or decreases based upon the adjustments (*e.g.,* increase for capital additions, like a transmission on a business truck, and decreases, like depreciation on a business truck, to arrive at the new adjusted basis).

alternative depreciation system (ADS). A method of depreciation that uses straight-line depreciation and results in a longer period of write-off than available under MACRS. (It is mandatory for foreign assets, luxury automobiles, and other such property.)

Alternative Minimum Tax (AMT). An alternative to the regular tax that is applied in lieu of the regular tax when positive adjustments and items of tax preference result in a greater tax than under the regular tax.

amortization. A deductible expense to recover the cost of an intangible asset (*e.g.*, patent).

amount realized. Actual amount received (*e.g.*, cash or property) upon the sale or exchange of property.

asset. An item of value. It may be tangible, intangible, or a natural resource.

at-risk limitations. Limitations on losses allowing for deductions only to the amount that a taxpayer has at risk in the activity (*e.g.*, a recourse note versus nonrecourse note).

B

basis. This is the cost of the asset or property, including any additions at the time of acquiring the asset or property additions (*e.g.*, installation costs) increase its basis.

C

capital asset. Property that is nonbusiness property (*e.g.*, personal property or investment property).

capital gain or loss. Gain or loss from sale or exchange of capital assets. It is arrived at by subtracting the adjusted basis from the amount realized.

cash method of accounting. A method of accounting that is based on reporting income and expenses when actually received and paid, respectively.

casualty loss. Losses from sudden casualties like fire, storm, earthquake, or other such occurrence.

child tax credit. Credit based on each qualifying child per taxpayer, provided the taxpayer's modified gross income is within certain thresholds.

D

deductions. Expenses that reduce gross income and result in adjusted gross income or taxable income.

deferred gain. Realized gain, but not recognized (taxable) until a later date.

dependency exemption. An exemption allowed a taxpayer for a qualifying dependent.

dependent. One who is supported by a taxpayer (generally over 50% support provided) to allow that taxpayer to claim a dependency exemption.

depreciable asset. Property used for business or held for production of income, provided the property has a useful life greater than one year.

depreciation. Known as cost recovery, a deductible expense that is for tangible personal property, provided it has a useful life greater than a year and is used for business purposes. Various depreciation methods (*e.g.*, straight-line, ACRS, MACRS) are used.

E

earned income. Payment for personal services as compensation.

earned income credit. Tax credit for qualified low income taxpayers.

exclusion. Any amount excluded from gross income (*e.g.*, gifts).

exemption. A deduction allowed a taxpayer (*e.g.*, itemized deductions).

F

fair market value. Standard used in tax, business, and accounting defined as the price that a willing buyer and a willing seller would accept if neither is under a compulsion to buy or sell.

fiscal year. A twelve-month consecutive period ending on the last day of a month other than December.

foreign tax credit. Tax credit allowed for income taxes paid to a foreign country.

G

gross income. Income from whatever sources before taking into account any deductions.

H

holding period. Length of time a taxpayer holds an asset. *See long-term capital gain or loss.*

home equity debt. Principal or secondary residence debt in excess of original acquisition debt.

I

Incentive Stock Option (ISO). Stock option received and exercised without recognition of income until stock under option is sold for regular tax purposes. Stock option exercised triggers a positive adjustment to compute AMTI for AMT purposes.

independent contractor. No control over the scope of taxpayer's duties and self-employed who files a Schedule C for tax purposes.

installment sale method of accounting. A method of accounting in which the gain reported as payments are received in lieu of a lump sum.

intangible personal property. Property with value denominated in rights as opposed to tangible substance.

itemized deductions. Expenses reported on Schedule A that reduce overall regular tax liability.

J

joint return. A regular tax return filed by a married couple that combines both their incomes and deductions.

L

long-term capital gain or loss. Gain or loss on the sale or exchange of a capital asset held greater than twelve months and taxed for regular tax at a preferential rate of 15% until 2008.

M

marginal tax rate. A federal statutory rate measured by each additional dollar of income over a federal statutory ceiling.

miscellaneous itemized deductions. Expenses treated as itemized deductions (*e.g.*, union dues, investment expenses, etc.) that must exceed 2% of AGI to be deductible.

modified accelerated cost recovery system (MACRS). A method of depreciation for assets or property acquired after 1986 that is a faster write-off than under straight-line depreciation. (*See ACRS.*)

N

net operating loss. Business expenses that exceed business revenues. It may be carried back two years or forward twenty years, and is limited as a tax deduction for AMT purposes.

O

ordinary income. Gain or loss on property other than from the sale or exchange of a capital asset or business

(Section 1231) asset. Taxed up to the maximum marginal tax rate (35%) and qualifies for AMTI purposes.

P

passive activity loss. Business loss from rental real estate or in which the taxpayer is not a material participant.

percentage depletion. A method of depletion for natural resources based upon a percentage of income from the natural resource.

Q

qualified residence interest. Interest that is deductible from acquisition debt or home equity debt. Strict limitations imposed for AMT purposes.

Qualified Small Business Stock (QSBS). Stock issued after August 10, 1993 that is held for more than five years. (Special exclusion rule for regular tax, but none for the AMT.)

R

realized gain or loss. The amount received for a property sold or exchanged, less the adjusted basis of that property.

S

Section 179 deduction. Individual taxpayer may elect to deduct rather than depreciate business property in the year the property is placed in service for the regular tax.

Section 1231 assets. Depreciable business property held for more than twelve months. Once the business property is sold or exchanged and any depreciation taken is recaptured, the balance is treated as capital gains.

short-term capital gain or loss. Gain or loss on the sale or exchange of a capital asset held for twelve months or less and taxed at ordinary rates up to 35% and subject to the AMT. *(See long-term capital gain or loss.)*

standard deduction. Federal tax deduction, adjusted for inflation, that reduces AGI and is taken in lieu of itemizing deductions for regular tax purposes. (Not allowed for AMT purposes.)

straight-line depreciation. A method of depreciation in which the cost of the asset is deducted uniformly at a constant rate over the useful life of the asset.

support. Payments made for a dependent (*e.g.*, food, shelter, clothing, etc.) that qualify the dependent under the support test for regular tax purposes.

T

tax-exempt income. Specifically excluded income for federal regular tax purposes (*e.g.*, municipal bond interest income). May be treated as a tax preference item if from a private activity bond under the AMT.

tax preference items. Items that must be included in AMTI to arrive at AMT. (No such classification for regular tax purposes.)

tax rate schedules. Issued each year by the IRS (see Publication No. 17) to calculate the individual income (regular) tax for taxable income amounts exceeding $100,000.

tax tables. Issued each year by the IRS (see Publication No. 17) to calculate the individual income (regular) tax for taxable income amounts of $100,000 or less.

taxable income. Gross income less all deductions and exemptions. Also known as the tax base upon which the regular tax is computed.

U

useful life. Estimate of the depreciable asset's life used in a trade or business.

appendix a:

Alternative Minimum Tax—Instructions and Form

This appendix contains the IRS instructions and Form 6251 for 2003. When this book went to press, the instructions for 2004 were not yet available. You can download the 2004 instructions from the IRS website, **www.irs.gov**.

As you can see by comparing the 2003 form with the 2004 form on page 15, the first page, Parts I and II, are nearly identical. The second page, Part III, has been simplified in 2004. Use this information to further understand how to calculate the AMT and complete Form 6251.

2003

Department of the Treasury
Internal Revenue Service

Instructions for Form 6251

Alternative Minimum Tax—Individuals

Section references are to the Internal Revenue Code.

General Instructions

Changes To Note

• For 2003, the exemption amount has increased to $40,250 ($58,000 if married filing jointly or qualifying widow(er); $29,000 if married filing separately).

• The 20% maximum tax rate on net capital gain has been reduced to 15%, and the 10% rate has been reduced to 5%, for sales and other dispositions after May 5, 2003 (and installment payments received after that date). See Part III.

• Beginning in 2003, your alternative tax net operating loss deduction (ATNOLD) is generally limited to 90% of your alternative minimum taxable income (figured without regard to the ATNOLD). See the line 27 instructions beginning on page 6.

• For 2003, the minimum exemption amount for a child under age 14 has increased to $5,600.

Purpose of Form

Use Form 6251 to figure the amount, if any, of your alternative minimum tax (AMT). The AMT applies to taxpayers who have certain types of income that receive special treatment, or who qualify for certain special deductions, under the tax law. Because of these special benefits, some taxpayers with substantial economic income can significantly reduce their regular tax. The AMT ensures that these taxpayers pay at least a minimum amount of tax.

Also use Form 6251 to figure the tax liability limit on the general business credit, the qualified electric vehicle credit, the nonconventional source fuel credit, or the credit for prior year minimum tax.

Who Must File

Attach Form 6251 to your return if:

• Line 31 is greater than line 34, **or**

• You claim any general business credit, the qualified electric vehicle credit, the nonconventional source fuel credit, or the credit for prior year minimum tax, **or**

• The total of lines 8 through 27 is negative and line 31 would be greater than line 34 if you did not take into account lines 8 through 27.

Recordkeeping

For the AMT, certain items of income, deductions, etc., receive different tax treatment than for the regular tax. Therefore, you need to refigure items for the AMT that you figured for the regular tax. In some cases, you may wish to do this by completing the applicable tax form a second time. If you do complete another form, **do not** attach it to your tax return (except for **Form 1116,** Foreign Tax Credit—see the instructions for line 32 beginning on page 7), but keep it for your records.

For the regular tax, some deductions and credits may result in carrybacks or carryforwards to other tax years. Examples are investment interest expense, a net operating loss, a capital loss, a passive activity loss, and the foreign tax credit. Because you may have to refigure these items for the AMT, the carryback or carryforward amount may be different for the AMT than for the regular tax. Your at-risk limits and basis amounts also may differ for the AMT. Therefore, you must keep records of these different amounts.

Partners and Shareholders

If you are a partner in a partnership or a shareholder in an S corporation, see Schedule K-1 and its instructions to figure your adjustments or preferences from the partnership or S corporation to include on Form 6251.

Nonresident Aliens

If you are a nonresident alien and you disposed of U.S. real property interests at a gain, you must make a special computation. Fill in Form 6251 through line 30. If your net gain from the disposition of U.S. real property interests and the amount on line 28 are **both** greater than the tentative amount you figured for line 30, replace the amount on line 30 with the smaller of that net gain or the amount on line 28. Also, write "RPI" on the dotted line next to line 30. Otherwise, do not change line 30.

Note: *If you are filing Form 1040NR, treat any reference in these instructions or on Form 6251 to a line on Form 1040 as a reference to the corresponding line on Form 1040NR.*

Credit for Prior Year Minimum Tax

See **Form 8801,** Credit for Prior Year Minimum Tax—Individuals, Estates, and Trusts, if you paid AMT for 2002 or you had a minimum tax credit carryforward on your 2002 Form 8801. If you pay AMT for 2003, you may be able to take a credit on Form 8801 for 2004.

Optional Write-Off for Certain Expenditures

There is no AMT adjustment for the following items if you elect for the regular tax to deduct them ratably over the period of time shown.

• Circulation expenditures—3 years (section 173).

• Research and experimental expenditures—10 years (section 174(a)).

• Mining exploration and development costs—10 years (sections 616(a) and 617(a)).

• Intangible drilling costs—60 months (section 263(c)).

See section 59(e) for more details.

Specific Instructions

CAUTION *If you claim the standard deduction on Form 1040, you must also use the standard deduction in figuring the AMT. However, if you owe AMT, you may be able to lower your total tax (regular tax **plus** AMT) by itemizing deductions on Form 1040.*

Part I—Alternative Minimum Taxable Income (AMTI)

CAUTION *To avoid duplication, any adjustment or preference for line 5, 18, or 19 or for a tax shelter farm activity on line 26 must not be taken into account in figuring the amount to enter for any other adjustment or preference.*

Line 1

If Form 1040, line 40, includes a write-in amount (such as a capital construction fund deduction for

Cat. No. 64277P

commercial fishermen), adjust line 1 by the write-in amount.

Line 3—Taxes

Do not include generation-skipping transfer taxes on income distributions.

Line 4—Certain Home Mortgage Interest

Include on this line home mortgage interest from line 10, 11, or 12 of Schedule A (Form 1040) **except** for interest on a mortgage whose proceeds were used to:

1. Buy, build, or substantially improve **(a)** your main home or **(b)** your second home that is a qualified dwelling (as defined below) or

2. Refinance a mortgage that meets the requirements of **1** above, but only to the extent that the refinanced amount did not exceed the balance of that mortgage immediately before the refinancing.

Exception. If the mortgage was taken out before July 1, 1982, **do not** include interest on the mortgage if it was secured by property that was your main home or a qualified dwelling used by you or a member of your family at the time the mortgage was taken out. See section 56(e)(3).

A **qualified dwelling** is any house, apartment, condominium, or mobile home not used on a transient basis.

Line 7—Refund of Taxes

Include any refund from Form 1040, line 10, that is attributable to state or local income taxes deducted after 1986. Also include any refunds received in 2003 and included in income on Form 1040, line 21, that are attributable to state or local personal property taxes, foreign income taxes, or state, local, or foreign real property taxes deducted after 1986. If you include an amount from line 21, you **must** write a description and the amount next to the entry space for line 7. For example, if you include a refund of real property taxes, write "real property" and the amount next to the entry space.

Line 8—Investment Interest

If you filled out **Form 4952,** Investment Interest Expense Deduction, for your regular tax, you will need to fill out a second Form 4952 for the AMT as follows.

Step 1. Follow the Form 4952 instructions for line 1, but also include the following amounts when completing line 1.

- Any interest expense on line 4 of Form 6251 that was paid or accrued on indebtedness attributable to property held for investment within the meaning of section 163(d)(5) (for example, interest on a home equity loan whose proceeds were invested in stocks or bonds).
- Any interest that would have been deductible if interest earned on private activity bonds issued after August 7, 1986, had been includible in gross income.

Step 2. Enter your **AMT** disallowed investment interest expense from 2002 on line 2. Complete line 3.

Step 3. When completing Part II, refigure the following amounts, taking into account all adjustments and preferences.

- Gross income from property held for investment.
- Net gain from the disposition of property held for investment.
- Net capital gain from the disposition of property held for investment.
- Investment expenses.

Include any interest income and investment expenses from private activity bonds issued after August 7, 1986.

Step 4. Complete Part III.

Enter on line 8 the difference between line 8 of your AMT Form 4952 and line 8 of your regular tax Form 4952. If your AMT expense is greater, enter the difference as a negative amount.

Note: *If you did not itemize deductions and you had investment interest expense, do not enter an amount on Form 6251, line 8, unless you reported investment interest expense on Schedule E. If you did, follow the steps above for completing Form 4952. Allocate the investment interest expense allowed on line 8 of the AMT Form 4952 in the same way you did for the regular tax. Enter on Form 6251, line 8, the difference between the amount allowed on Schedule E for the regular tax and the amount allowed on Schedule E for the AMT.*

Line 9—Depletion

You must refigure your depletion deduction for the AMT. To do so, use only income and deductions allowed for the AMT when refiguring the limit based on taxable income from the property under section 613(a) and the limit based on taxable income, with certain adjustments, under section 613A(d)(1). Also, your depletion deduction for mines, wells, and other natural deposits under section 611 is limited to the property's adjusted basis at the end of the year, as refigured for the AMT, unless you are an independent producer or royalty owner claiming percentage depletion for oil and gas wells under section 613A(c). Figure this limit separately for each property. When refiguring the property's adjusted basis, take into account any AMT adjustments you made this year or in previous years that affect basis (other than current year depletion).

Enter the difference between the regular tax and AMT deduction. If the AMT deduction is greater, enter the difference as a negative amount.

Line 11—Interest From Private Activity Bonds

Enter on line 11 interest you earned on "specified private activity bonds" reduced (but not below zero) by any deduction that would have been allowable if the interest were includible in gross income for the regular tax. Generally, the term "specified private activity bond" means any private activity bond (as defined in section 141) issued after August 7, 1986. See section 57(a)(5) for exceptions and more details.

Exempt-interest dividends paid by a regulated investment company are treated as interest income on specified private activity bonds to the extent the dividends are attributable to interest on the bonds received by the company, minus an allocable share of the expenses paid or incurred by the company in earning the interest.

If you are filing **Form 8814,** Parents' Election To Report Child's Interest and Dividends, any tax-exempt interest income from line 1b of that form that is a preference item must be included on this line.

Line 12—Qualified Small Business Stock

If you claimed the exclusion under section 1202 for gain on qualified small business stock held more than 5 years, compute the amount to enter on line 12 as follows.

- If you sold qualified small business stock before May 6, 2003, multiply the excluded gain (as shown on Schedule D (Form 1040)) by 42% (.42).
- If you sold qualified small business stock after May 5, 2003, multiply the excluded gain (as shown on Schedule D (Form 1040)) by 7% (.07).

Combine the results and enter on line 12 as a positive amount.

Line 13—Exercise of Incentive Stock Options

For the regular tax, no income is recognized when an incentive stock option (ISO), as defined in section 422(b), is exercised. However, this rule does not apply for the AMT. Instead, you generally must include on line 13 the excess, if any, of:

- The fair market value of the stock acquired through exercise of the option (determined without regard to any lapse restriction) when your rights in the acquired stock first become transferable or when these rights are no longer subject to a substantial risk of forfeiture **over**
- The amount you paid for the stock, including any amount you paid for the ISO used to acquire the stock.

Note: *Even if your rights in the stock are not transferable and are subject to a substantial risk of forfeiture, you may elect to include in AMT income the excess of the stock's fair market value* *(determined without regard to any lapse restriction) over the exercise price upon the transfer to you of the stock acquired through exercise of the option. You must make the election by the 30th day after the date of the transfer. See* ***Pub. 525,*** *Taxable and Nontaxable Income, for more details.*

If you acquired stock by exercising an ISO and you disposed of that stock in the same year, the tax treatment under the regular tax and the AMT is the same, and no adjustment is required.

Increase your AMT basis in any stock acquired through the exercise of an ISO by the amount of the adjustment. Keep adequate records for both the AMT and regular tax so that you may figure your adjustment. See the instructions for line 16.

Line 15—Large Partnerships

If you were a partner in an electing large partnership, enter the amount from Schedule K-1 (Form 1065-B), box 6. Take into account any amount from box 5 on Form 6251, line 18.

Line 16—Disposition of Property

Use this line to report any AMT adjustment related to the disposition of property resulting from refiguring:

1. Gain or loss from the sale, exchange, or involuntary conversion of property reported on **Form 4797,** Sales of Business Property;

2. Casualty gain or loss to business or income-producing property reported on **Form 4684,** Casualties and Thefts;

3. Ordinary income from the disposition of property not already taken into account in **1** or **2** above or on any other line on Form 6251, such as a disqualifying disposition of stock acquired in a prior year by exercising an incentive stock option; and

4. Capital gain or loss (including any carryover that is different for the AMT) reported on **Schedule D** (Form 1040), Capital Gains and Losses.

CAUTION *The $3,000 capital loss limitation for the regular tax applies* ***separately*** *for the AMT. See the instructions and example below.*

First figure any ordinary income adjustment related to **3** above. Then, refigure Form 4684, Form 4797, and Schedule D for the AMT, if applicable, by taking into account any adjustments you made this year or in previous years that affect your basis or otherwise result in a different amount for the AMT. If you have a capital loss after refiguring Schedule D for the AMT, apply the $3,000 capital loss limitation separately to the AMT loss. For each of the four items listed above, figure the difference between the amount included in taxable income for the regular tax and the amount included in income for the AMT. Treat the difference as a negative amount if **(a)** both the AMT and regular tax amounts are zero or more and the AMT amount is less than the regular tax amount or **(b)** the AMT amount is a loss, and the regular tax amount is a smaller loss or zero or more.

Enter on line 16 the combined adjustments for the 4 items above.

Example. On March 13, 2002, Victor Ash, whose filing status is single, paid $20,000 to exercise an incentive stock option (which was granted to him on January 2, 2001) to buy 200 shares of stock worth $200,000. The $180,000 difference between his cost and the value of the stock at the time he exercised the option is not taxable for the regular tax. His regular tax basis in the stock at the end of 2002 is $20,000. For the AMT, however, Ash must include the $180,000 as an adjustment on his 2002 Form 6251. His AMT basis in the stock at the end of 2002 is $200,000.

On January 20, 2003, Ash sold 100 of the shares for $75,000. Because Ash did not hold these shares more than 1 year, that sale is a disqualifying disposition. For the regular tax, Ash has ordinary income of $65,000 (proceeds minus his $10,000 basis in the 100 shares). Ash has no capital gain or loss for the regular tax resulting from the sale. For the AMT, Ash has no ordinary income, but has a short-term capital loss of $25,000 (proceeds minus his $100,000 AMT basis in the 100 shares).

On April 21, 2003, Ash sold the other 100 shares for $60,000. Because he held the shares for more than 1 year, the sale is not a disqualifying disposition. For the regular tax, Ash has a long-term capital gain of $50,000 (proceeds minus his regular tax basis of $10,000). For the AMT, Ash has a long-term capital loss of $40,000 (proceeds minus his AMT basis of $100,000).

Ash has no other sales of stock or other capital assets for 2003. Ash enters a total negative adjustment of $118,000 on line 16 of his 2003 Form 6251, figured as follows:

- Ash figures a negative adjustment of $65,000 for the difference between the $65,000 of regular tax ordinary income and the $0 of AMT ordinary income for the first sale.
- For the regular tax, Ash has $50,000 capital gain net income reported on Schedule D for the second sale. For the AMT, Ash has a $25,000 short-term capital loss from the first sale, and a $40,000 long-term capital loss from the second sale, resulting in a net capital loss of $65,000 for the AMT. However, only $3,000 of the $65,000 net capital loss is allowed for 2003 for the AMT. The difference between the regular tax Schedule D gain of $50,000 and the $3,000 loss allowed for the AMT results in a $53,000 negative adjustment to include on line 16.

Ash has an AMT capital loss carryover from 2003 to 2004 of $62,000, of which $22,000 is short-term and $40,000 is long-term. If he has no other Schedule D transactions for 2004, his adjustment reported on line 16 of his 2004 Form 6251 would be limited to ($3,000), the amount of his capital loss limitation for 2004.

Line 17—Post-1986 Depreciation

This section describes when depreciation must be refigured for the AMT and how to figure the amount to enter on line 17.

Do not use line 17 for depreciation related to the following.

- Employee business expenses claimed on line 20 of Schedule A (Form 1040). Take this adjustment into account on line 5.
- Passive activities. Take this adjustment into account on line 18.
- An activity for which you are not at risk or income or loss from a partnership or an S corporation if the basis limitations apply. Take this adjustment into account on line 19.
- A tax shelter farm activity. Take this adjustment into account on line 26.

What Depreciation Must Be Refigured for the AMT?

Generally, you must refigure depreciation for the AMT, including depreciation allocable to inventory costs, for:

- Property placed in service after 1998 that is depreciated for the regular tax using the 200% declining balance method (generally 3-, 5-, 7-, and 10-year property under the modified accelerated cost recovery system (MACRS), except for qualified property eligible for the special depreciation allowance (see page 4));
- Section 1250 property placed in service after 1998 that is **not** depreciated for the regular tax using the straight line method; and
- Tangible property placed in service after 1986 and before 1999 (if the transitional election was made under section 203(a)(1)(B) of the Tax Reform Act of 1986, this rule applies to property placed in service after July 31, 1986).

What Depreciation Is Not Refigured for the AMT?

Do not refigure depreciation for the AMT for the following.

- Residential rental property placed in service after 1998.
- Nonresidential real property with a class life of 27.5 years or more placed in service after 1998 that is depreciated for the regular tax using the straight line method.
- Other section 1250 property placed in service after 1998 that is depreciated for the regular tax using the straight line method.

- Property (other than section 1250 property) placed in service after 1998 that is depreciated for the regular tax using the 150% declining balance method or the straight line method.
- Property for which you elected to use the alternative depreciation system (ADS) of section 168(g) for the regular tax.
- Property that is qualified property under section 168(k)(2) or 168(k)(4) (property eligible for the special depreciation allowance). The special allowance is deductible for the AMT, and there also is no adjustment required for any depreciation figured on the remaining basis of the qualified property. Property for which an election is in effect under section 168(k)(2)(C)(iii) to not have the special allowance apply is **not** qualified property. See the Instructions for Form 4562 for the definition of qualified property.
- Any part of the cost of any property for which you made the election under section 179 to treat the cost of the property as a deductible expense. The reduction to the depreciable basis of section 179 property by the amount of the section 179 expense deduction is the same for the regular tax and the AMT.
- Motion picture films, videotapes, or sound recordings.
- Property depreciated under the unit-of-production method or any other method not expressed in a term of years.
- Qualified Indian reservation property.
- Qualified revitalization expenditures for a building for which you elected to claim the commercial revitalization deduction under section 1400I.

How Is Depreciation Refigured for the AMT?

Property placed in service before 1999. Refigure depreciation for the AMT using ADS, with the same convention used for the regular tax. See the table below for the method and recovery period to use.

Property Placed in Service Before 1999	
IF the property is...	**THEN use the...**
Section 1250 property.	Straight line method over 40 years.
Tangible property (other than section 1250 property) depreciated using straight line for the regular tax.	Straight line method over the property's AMT class life.
Any other tangible property.	150% declining balance method, switching to straight line the first tax year it gives a larger deduction, over the property's AMT class life.

Property placed in service after 1998. Use the same convention and recovery period used for the regular tax. For property other than section 1250 property, use the 150% declining balance method, switching to straight line the first tax year it gives a larger deduction. For section 1250 property, use the straight line method.

How Is the AMT Class Life Determined?

The class life used for the AMT is not necessarily the same as the recovery period used for the regular tax. The class lives for the AMT are listed in Rev. Proc. 87-56, 1987-2 C.B. 674, and in **Pub. 946,** How To Depreciate Property. Use 12 years for any tangible personal property not assigned a class life.

TIP *See Pub. 946 for optional tables that may be used to figure AMT depreciation. Rev. Proc. 89-15, 1989-1 C.B. 816, has special rules for short years and for property disposed of before the end of the recovery period.*

How Is the Adjustment Figured?

Subtract the AMT deduction for depreciation from the regular tax deduction and enter the result. If the AMT deduction is more than the regular tax deduction, enter the difference as a negative amount.

In addition to the AMT adjustment to your deduction for depreciation, you must also adjust the amount of depreciation that was capitalized, if any, to account for the difference between the rules for the regular tax and the AMT. Include on this line the current year adjustment to taxable income, if any, resulting from the difference.

Line 18—Passive Activities

Your passive activity gains and losses must be refigured for the AMT by taking into account all adjustments and preferences and any AMT prior year unallowed losses that apply to that activity. You may fill out a second **Form 8582,** Passive Activity Loss Limitations, and the other forms or schedules on which your passive activities are reported, to determine your passive activity loss allowed for the AMT, but **do not** file the second set of forms and schedules with your tax return.

Example. You are a partner in a partnership and the Schedule K-1 (Form 1065) you received shows the following.
- A passive activity loss of $4,125,
- A depreciation adjustment of $500 on post-1986 property, and
- An adjustment of $225 on the disposition of property.

Because the two adjustments above are not allowed for the AMT, you must first reduce the passive activity loss by those amounts. The result is a passive activity loss for the AMT of $3,400. You then enter this amount on the AMT Form 8582 and refigure the allowable passive activity loss for the AMT.

Note: *The amount of any AMT passive activity loss that is not deductible and is carried forward is likely to differ from the regular tax amount, if any. Therefore, keep adequate records for both the AMT and regular tax.*

Enter the difference between the amount that would be reported for the activity on Schedule C, C-EZ, E, or F or **Form 4835,** Farm Rental Income and Expenses, for the AMT and the regular tax amount. If **(a)** the AMT loss is more than the regular tax loss, **(b)** the AMT gain is less than the regular tax gain, **or (c)** you have an AMT loss and a regular tax gain, enter the adjustment as a negative amount.

Enter any adjustment for amounts reported on Schedule D, Form 4684, or Form 4797 for the activity on line 16 instead of line 18. See the instructions for line 16.

Publicly Traded Partnership (PTP)

If you had a loss from a PTP, refigure the loss using any AMT adjustments and preferences and any AMT prior year unallowed loss.

Tax Shelter Passive Farm Activities

Refigure any gain or loss from a tax shelter passive farm activity taking into account all AMT adjustments and preferences and any AMT prior year unallowed losses. If the amount is a gain, include it on the AMT Form 8582. If the amount is a loss, do not include it on the AMT Form 8582. Carry the loss forward to 2004 to see if you have a gain or loss from tax shelter passive farm activities for 2004.

Insolvency

If at the end of the tax year your liabilities exceed the fair market value of your assets, increase your passive activity loss allowed by that excess (but not by more than your total loss). See section 58(c)(1).

Line 19—Loss Limitations

For passive activities, see the line 18 instructions on this page instead. For tax shelter farm activities (that are not passive), see the line 26 instructions beginning on page 5.

Refigure your gains and losses from activities for which you are not at risk and basis limitations applicable to partnerships and S corporations by taking into account all AMT adjustments and preferences that apply. See sections 59(h), 465, 704(d), and 1366(d).

Enter the difference between the amount that would be reported for the activity on Schedule C, C-EZ, E, or F or Form 4835 for the AMT and the regular tax amount. If **(a)** the AMT loss is more than the regular tax loss, **or (b)** the

AMT gain is less than the regular tax gain, **or (c)** you have an AMT loss and a regular tax gain, enter the adjustment as a negative amount.

The AMT amount of any gain or loss from activities for which you are not at risk is likely to differ from the regular tax amount. Your AMT basis in partnerships and S corporations is also likely to differ from your regular tax basis. Therefore, keep adequate records for both the AMT and regular tax.

Enter any adjustment for amounts reported on Schedule D, Form 4684, or Form 4797 for the activity on line 16 instead.

Line 20—Circulation Costs

Note: *Do not make this adjustment for costs for which you elected the optional 3-year write-off for the regular tax.*

Circulation costs (expenditures to establish, maintain, or increase the circulation of a newspaper, magazine, or other periodical) deducted in full for the regular tax in the year they were paid or incurred must be capitalized and amortized over 3 years for the AMT. Enter the difference between the regular tax and AMT deduction. If the AMT deduction is greater, enter the difference as a negative amount.

If you had a loss on property for which circulation costs have not been fully amortized for the AMT, your AMT deduction is the **smaller** of **(a)** the amount of the loss allowable for the costs had they remained capitalized or **(b)** the remaining costs to be amortized for the AMT.

Line 21—Long-Term Contracts

For the AMT, you generally must use the percentage-of-completion method described in section 460(b) to determine your income from any long-term contract (defined in section 460(f)). However, this rule does not apply to any home construction contract (as defined in section 460(e)(6)). For contracts excepted from the percentage-of-completion method for the regular tax by section 460(e)(1), you must use the simplified procedures for allocating costs outlined in section 460(b)(3) to determine the percentage of completion.

Enter the difference between the AMT and regular tax income. If the AMT income is smaller, enter the difference as a negative amount.

Note: *If you are required to use the percentage-of-completion method for either the regular tax or the AMT, you may owe or be entitled to a refund of interest for the tax year the contract is completed or adjusted. For details, see **Form 8697,** Interest Computation Under the Look-Back Method for Completed Long-Term Contracts.*

Line 22—Mining Costs

Note: *Do not make this adjustment for costs for which you elected the optional 10-year write-off for the regular tax.*

Mining exploration and development costs deducted in full for the regular tax in the tax year they were paid or incurred must be capitalized and amortized over 10 years for the AMT. Enter the difference between the regular tax and AMT deduction. If the AMT deduction is greater, enter the difference as a negative amount.

If you had a loss on property for which mining costs have not been fully amortized for the AMT, your AMT deduction is the smaller of **(a)** the loss allowable for the costs had they remained capitalized or **(b)** the remaining costs to be amortized for the AMT.

Line 23—Research and Experimental Costs

Note: *Do not make this adjustment for costs paid or incurred in connection with an activity in which you materially participated under the passive activity rules or for costs for which you elected the optional 10-year write-off for the regular tax.*

Research and experimental costs deducted in full for the regular tax in the tax year they were paid or incurred must be capitalized and amortized over 10 years for the AMT. Enter the difference between the regular tax and AMT deduction. If the AMT deduction is greater, enter the difference as a negative amount.

If you had a loss on property for which research and experimental costs have not been fully amortized for the AMT, your AMT deduction is the smaller of **(a)** the loss allowable for the costs had they remained capitalized or **(b)** the remaining costs to be amortized for the AMT.

Line 24—Installment Sales

The installment method does not apply for the AMT to any nondealer disposition of property after August 16, 1986, but before January 1, 1987, if an installment obligation to which the proportionate disallowance rule applied arose from the disposition. Enter on line 24 the amount of installment sale income reported for the regular tax.

Line 25—Intangible Drilling Costs (IDCs)

Note: *Do not make this adjustment for costs for which you elected the optional 60-month write-off for the regular tax.*

IDCs from oil, gas, and geothermal wells are a preference to the extent that the excess IDCs exceed 65% of the net income from the wells. Figure the preference for all oil and gas properties separately from the preference for all geothermal properties.

Figure **excess IDCs** as follows.

Step 1. Determine the amount of your IDCs allowed for the regular tax under section 263(c), but do not include any section 263(c) deduction for nonproductive wells.

Step 2. Subtract the amount that would have been allowed had you amortized these IDCs over a 120-month period starting with the month the well was placed in production.

Note: *If you prefer not to use the 120-month period, you may elect to use any method that is permissible in determining cost depletion.*

Determine **net income** by reducing the gross income that you received or accrued during the tax year from all oil, gas, and geothermal wells by the deductions allocable to those wells (reduced by the excess IDCs). When refiguring net income, use only income and deductions allowed for the AMT.

Exception. The preference for IDCs from oil and gas wells does not apply to taxpayers who are independent producers (that is, not integrated oil companies as defined in section 291(b)(4)). However, this benefit may be limited. First, figure the IDC preference as if this exception did not apply. Then, for purposes of this exception, complete Form 6251 through line 26, including the IDC preference, and combine lines 1 through 26. If the amount of the IDC preference exceeds 40% of the total of lines 1 through 26, enter the excess on line 25 (your benefit from this exception is limited). Otherwise, do not enter an amount on line 25 (your benefit from this exception is not limited).

Line 26—Other Adjustments

Enter on line 26 the total of any other adjustments that apply to you, including the following.

Depreciation Figured Using Pre-1987 Rules

Note: *This preference generally only applies to property placed in service after 1987, but depreciated using pre-1987 rules due to transitional provisions of the Tax Reform Act of 1986.*

For the AMT, you must use the straight line method to figure depreciation on real property for which accelerated depreciation was determined using pre-1987 rules. Use a recovery period of 19 years for 19-year real property and 15 years for low-income housing. For leased personal property other than recovery property, enter the amount by which your regular tax depreciation using the pre-1987 rules exceeds the depreciation allowable using the straight line method. For leased 10-year recovery property and leased 15-year public utility property, enter the amount by which your regular tax depreciation exceeds the depreciation allowable using the straight line method with a half-year convention, no salvage value, and a recovery period of 15 years (22 years for 15-year public utility property).

Figure the excess of the regular tax depreciation over the AMT depreciation separately for each property and include on line 26 only positive amounts.

Patron's Adjustment

Distributions you received from a cooperative may be includible in income. Unless the distributions are nontaxable, include on line 26 the total AMT patronage dividend adjustment reported to you by the cooperative.

Pollution Control Facilities

The section 169 election to amortize the basis of a certified pollution control facility over a 60-month period is not available for the AMT. For facilities placed in service before 1999, figure the AMT deduction using ADS. For facilities placed in service after 1998, figure the AMT deduction under MACRS using the straight line method. Enter the difference between the regular tax and AMT deduction. If the AMT amount is greater, enter the difference as a negative amount.

Tax Shelter Farm Activities

Figure this adjustment only if you have a gain or loss from a tax shelter farm activity (as defined in section 58(a)(2)) that is **not** a passive activity. If the activity **is** passive, you must include it with your other passive activities on line 18.

Refigure all gains and losses you reported for the regular tax from tax shelter farm activities by taking into account any AMT adjustments and preferences. Determine your tax shelter farm activity gain or loss for the AMT using the same rules you used for the regular tax with the following modifications. No refigured loss is allowed, except to the extent you are insolvent (see section 58(c)(1)). A refigured loss may not be used in the current tax year to offset gains from other tax shelter farm activities. Instead, any refigured loss must be suspended and carried forward indefinitely until **(a)** you have a gain in a subsequent tax year from that same activity **or (b)** you dispose of the activity.

Enter the difference between the amount that would be reported for the activity on Schedule E or F or Form 4835 for the AMT and the regular tax amount. If **(a)** the AMT loss is more than the regular tax loss, **(b)** the AMT gain is less than the regular tax gain, **or (c)** you have an AMT loss and a regular tax gain, enter the adjustment as a negative amount.

Enter any adjustment for amounts reported on Schedule D, Form 4684, or Form 4797 for the activity on line 16 instead.

Charitable Contributions of Certain Property

If you made a charitable contribution of property to which section 170(e) applies and you had a different basis for AMT purposes, you may have to make an adjustment. See section 170(e) for details.

Alcohol Fuel Credit

If your taxable income includes an amount from the alcohol fuel credit under section 87, include that amount as a negative amount on line 26.

Related Adjustments

If you have an entry on line 8 because you deducted investment interest allocable to an interest in a trade or business, or on line 9, 12, 13, or 15 through 25, or you have any amount included on line 26 from pre-1987 depreciation, patron's adjustment, pollution control facilities, or tax shelter farm activities, you may have to refigure any item of income or deduction based on a limit of income **other than** AGI or modified AGI.

Affected items include the following.

- Section 179 expense deduction (Form 4562, line 12).
- Expenses for business or rental use of your home.
- Conservation expenses (Schedule F, line 14).
- Taxable IRA distributions (Form 1040, line 15b), if prior year IRA deductions were different for the AMT and the regular tax.
- Self-employed health insurance deduction (Form 1040, line 29).
- Self-employed SEP, SIMPLE, and qualified plans deduction (Form 1040, line 30).
- IRA deduction (Form 1040, line 24), affected by the earned income limitation of section 219(b)(1)(B).

Figure the difference between the AMT and regular tax amount for each item. Combine the amounts for all your related adjustments and include the total on line 26. Keep a copy of all computations for your records, including any AMT carryover and basis amounts.

Note: *Do not include on line 26 any adjustment for an item you refigured on another line of this form (for example, line 9).*

Example. On your Schedule C (Form 1040) you have a net profit of $9,000 before figuring your section 179 deduction (and you do not report any other business income on your return). During the year, you purchased an asset for $10,000 for which you elect to take the section 179 deduction. You also have an AMT depreciation adjustment of $700 for other assets depreciated on your Schedule C.

Your section 179 deduction for the regular tax is limited to your net profit (before any section 179 deduction) of $9,000. The $1,000 excess is a section 179 deduction carryforward for the regular tax.

For the AMT, your net profit is $9,700, and you are allowed a section 179 deduction of $9,700 for the AMT. You have a section 179 deduction carryforward of $300 for the AMT.

You include a $700 negative adjustment on line 26 because your section 179 deduction for the AMT is $700 greater than your allowable regular tax deduction. In the following year, when you use the $1,000 regular tax carryforward, you will have a $700 positive related adjustment for the AMT because your AMT carryforward is only $300.

Line 27—Alternative Tax Net Operating Loss Deduction (ATNOLD)

The ATNOLD is the sum of the alternative tax net operating loss (ATNOL) carryovers and carrybacks to the tax year, subject to the limitation explained below. Figure your ATNOLD as follows.

Your ATNOL for a loss year is the excess of the deductions allowed for figuring AMTI (excluding the ATNOLD) over the income included in AMTI. Figure this excess with the modifications in section 172(d), taking into account the adjustments in sections 56 and 58 and preferences in section 57 (that is, the section 172(d) modifications must be separately figured for the ATNOL). For example, the limitation of nonbusiness deductions to the amount of nonbusiness income must be separately figured for the ATNOL, using only nonbusiness income and deductions that are included in AMTI.

Your ATNOLD may be limited. To figure the ATNOLD limitation, you must first figure your AMTI without regard to the ATNOLD. To do this, first figure a tentative amount for line 9 by treating line 27 as if it were zero. Next, figure a tentative total of lines 1 through 26 using the tentative line 9 amount and treating line 27 as if it were zero. Your ATNOLD limitation is 90% of this tentative total.

Enter on line 27 the smaller of the ATNOLD or the ATNOLD limitation.

Any ATNOL not used may be carried back 2 years or forward up to 20 years (15 years for loss years beginning before 1998). In some cases, the carryback period is longer than 2 years; see section 172(b) for details. The treatment of ATNOLs does not affect your regular tax NOL.

Note: *If you elected under section 172(b)(3) to forego the carryback period for the regular tax, the election also applies for the AMT.*

Line 28—Alternative Minimum Taxable Income

If your filing status is married filing separately and line 28 is more than $191,000, you must include an additional amount on line 28. If line 28 is $307,000 or more, include an additional $29,000. Otherwise, include 25% of the excess of the amount on line 28 over $191,000. For example, if the amount on line 28 is $211,000, enter $216,000 instead—the additional $5,000 is 25% of $20,000 ($211,000 minus $191,000).

Special Rule for Holders of a Residual Interest in a REMIC

If you held a residual interest in a real estate mortgage investment conduit (REMIC) in 2003, the amount you enter on line 28 may not be less than the amount on Schedule E, line 38, column (c). If the amount in column (c) is larger than the amount you would otherwise enter on line 28, enter the amount from column (c) instead and write "Sch. Q" on the dotted line next to line 28.

Part II—Alternative Minimum Tax

Line 29—Exemption Amount

If line 28 is more than the amount shown for your filing status in the middle column of the chart on line 29, see the worksheet on this page to figure the amount to enter on line 29.

Child Under Age 14

If this form is for a child under age 14, complete the worksheet on this page. A **child under age 14** is a child who was born after January 1, 1990, and at least one of whose parents was alive at the end of 2003.

Line 8 of the worksheet. Earned income includes wages, tips, and other amounts received for personal services performed. If the child is engaged as a sole proprietor or as a partner in a trade or business in which both personal services and capital are material income-producing factors, earned income also includes a reasonable allowance for compensation for personal services rendered by the child, but not more than 30% of his or her share of the net profits from that trade or business (after subtracting the deduction for one-half of self-employment tax). However, the 30% limit does not apply if there are no net profits from the trade or business. If capital is not an income-producing factor and the child's personal services produced the business income, all of the child's gross income from the trade or business is considered earned income.

Line 32—Alternative Minimum Tax Foreign Tax Credit (AMTFTC)

TIP *To see if you need to figure your AMTFTC, fill in line 34 of Form 6251 as instructed (you will first need to figure your foreign tax credit for the regular tax and complete Form 1040, line 44). If the amount on line 34 is greater than or equal to the amount on line 31, you do not owe the AMT. Enter zero on line 35 and see **Who Must File** on page 1 to find out if you must attach Form 6251 to your return. However, even if you do not owe the AMT, you may need to complete line 32 to see if you have an AMTFTC carryback or carryforward to other tax years.*

Your AMTFTC is your foreign tax credit refigured as follows.

1. Use a separate AMT Form 1116 for each separate limitation category specified at the top of Form 1116. Write "AMT" in the top margin of each Form 1116.

Note: *When applying the separate limitation categories, use the applicable AMT rate instead of the regular tax rate to determine if any income is "high-taxed."*

2. If you previously made or are making the **simplified limitation election** (see page 8), skip Part I and enter on the AMT Form 1116, line 16, the same amount you entered on that line for the regular tax. If you did not complete Form 1116 for the regular tax and you previously made or are making the simplified limitation election, complete Part I and lines 14 through 16 of the AMT Form 1116 using regular tax amounts.

If the election does not apply, complete Part I using only income and deductions that are allowed for the AMT and attributable to sources outside the United States. If required by the Instructions for Form 1116 (based on your AMT Schedule D), complete Worksheet A, Worksheet B, and the Worksheet for Line 17 for the AMT. (But, if required, make adjustments to your foreign source capital gains and losses using the instructions in **Pub. 514,** Foreign Tax Credit for Individuals, instead of completing Worksheets A and B.) If you are required to complete an AMT Worksheet for Line 17, follow the instructions under **5** beginning below.

3. Complete Part II and lines 9 through 13 of the AMT Form 1116. Use your AMTFTC carryover, if any, on line 10.

4. If the simplified limitation election does not apply, complete lines 14 through 16 of the AMT Form 1116.

5. If you did not complete Schedule D (Form 1040) for the regular tax and did not complete Part III of Form 6251, enter the AMTI from Form 6251, line 28, on line 17 of the AMT Form 1116 and go to **6** below. Otherwise, follow these steps to complete, for the AMT, the Worksheet for Line 17 in the Form 1116 instructions.

a. Enter the amount from Form 6251, line 28, on line 1 of the AMT Worksheet for Line 17.

b. Complete a Schedule D for the AMT as explained in the instructions for lines 37, 38, 39, 43, and 46 on page 8 (or, if you already completed an AMT Schedule D to complete Part III of Form 6251, use that Schedule D). Next, enter the amount from Form 6251, line 30, on line 21 of your AMT Schedule D or line 1 of the AMT Schedule D Tax Worksheet. Then, complete lines 27

Exemption Worksheet—Line 29

Keep for Your Records

Note: *If Form 6251, line 28, is equal to or more than: $273,500 if single or head of household; $382,000 if married filing jointly or qualifying widow(er); or $191,000 if married filing separately; your exemption is zero.* ***Do not*** *complete this worksheet; instead, enter the amount from Form 6251, line 28, on line 30 and go to line 31.*

1.	Enter: $40,250 if single or head of household; $58,000 if married filing jointly or qualifying widow(er); $29,000 if married filing separately		**1.**	
2.	Enter your alternative minimum taxable income (AMTI) from Form 6251, line 28	**2.**		
3.	Enter: $112,500 if single or head of household; $150,000 if married filing jointly or qualifying widow(er); $75,000 if married filing separately	**3.**		
4.	Subtract line 3 from line 2. If zero or less, enter -0-	**4.**		
5.	Multiply line 4 by 25% (.25)		**5.**	
6.	Subtract line 5 from line 1. If zero or less, enter -0-. If this form is for a child under age 14, go to line 7 below. Otherwise, **stop here** and enter this amount on Form 6251, line 29, and go to Form 6251, line 30		▶ **6.**	
7.	Child's minimum exemption amount		**7.**	$5,600
8.	Enter the **child's earned income,** if any (see instructions)		**8.**	
9.	Add lines 7 and 8		**9.**	
10.	Enter the **smaller** of line 6 or line 9 here and on Form 6251, line 29, and go to Form 6251, line 30		▶ **10.**	

through 48 of the AMT Schedule D (you may skip lines 33, 37, 39, and 47) or lines 14 through 46 of the AMT Schedule D Tax Worksheet (you may skip lines 22, 26, 28, 36, 38, and 44).

c. Complete the rest of the AMT Worksheet for Line 17 using amounts from the AMT Schedule D or AMT Schedule D Tax Worksheet.

6. Enter the amount from Form 6251, line 31, on the AMT Form 1116, line 19. Complete lines 18, 20, and 21 of the AMT Form 1116.

7. Complete Part IV of the **first** AMT Form 1116 only.

Follow the instructions below to figure the amount to enter on Form 6251, line 32.

If you have no entry on Form 6251, line 27, and no intangible drilling costs (IDCs) (or the exception for IDCs does not apply to you—see the instructions for line 25 on page 5), enter on Form 6251, line 32, the **smaller** of:

- 90% of Form 6251, line 31, or
- The amount from line 33 of the first AMT Form 1116.

If you have an entry on line 27 or the exception for IDCs applies to you:

1. Figure the amount of tax that would be on line 31 if line 27 were zero and the exception did not apply,

2. Multiply the amount from **1** above by 10%,

3. Subtract the amount from **2** above from the tax on line 31, and

4. Enter on Form 6251, line 32, the **smaller** of the amount from **3** above or the amount from line 33 of the first AMT Form 1116.

Attach to your tax return, after Form 6251, all AMT Forms 1116 you used to figure your AMTFTC.

AMTFTC Carryback and Carryforward

If your AMTFTC is limited, the unused amount may be carried back or forward according to sections 59(a)(2)(B) and 904(c).

Simplified Limitation Election

You may elect to use a simplified section 904 limitation to figure your AMTFTC. If you do, use your regular tax income for Form 1116, Part I, instead of refiguring your foreign source income for the AMT, as described earlier. You must make the election for the first tax year after 1997 for which you claim an AMTFTC. If you do not make the election for that year, you may not make it for a later year. Once made, the election applies to all later tax years and may be revoked only with IRS consent.

Part III—Tax Computation Using Maximum Capital Gains Rates

Lines 37, 38, 39, 43, and 46

If you **did not** complete Schedule D (Form 1040) but you figured your tax using the **Qualified Dividends and Capital Gain Tax Worksheet** in the instructions for line 41 of Form 1040, then:

- Enter on Form 6251, lines 37 and 39, the amount from line 6 of that worksheet;
- Skip Form 6251, line 38;
- Enter on Form 6251, line 43, the amount, if any, from line 10 of the worksheet; and
- Enter on Form 6251, line 46, the amount, if any, from line 11 of the worksheet (or if that line is blank, the amount from line 19 of the worksheet).

If you did complete Schedule D, you generally may use the amounts from Schedule D or the Schedule D Tax Worksheet as instructed on Form 6251, lines 37, 38, 39, and 46. But **do not** use those amounts if either of the following applies.

1. Any gain or loss on Schedule D is different for the AMT (for example, because of a different basis for the AMT due to depreciation adjustments, an incentive stock option adjustment, or a different AMT capital loss carryover from 2002).

2. You did not complete Part IV of Schedule D because Form 1040, line 40, is zero.

If **1** or **2** above applies, complete a Schedule D for the AMT as follows. If **1** applies, refigure the amounts for Schedule D, Parts I, II, and III for the AMT; otherwise, use the regular tax amounts. Next, complete lines 19, 22 through 26, and 31 of the AMT Schedule D (or lines 2 through 13, plus line 20, of an AMT Schedule D Tax Worksheet, if applicable). Use amounts from the AMT Schedule D or AMT Schedule D Tax Worksheet to complete lines 37, 38, 39, and 46 of Form 6251. Keep the AMT Schedule D and worksheet for your records, but **do not** attach the AMT Schedule D to your tax return.

If you did not complete line 30 of Schedule D for the regular tax (or line 19 of the Schedule D Tax Worksheet, if applicable), enter zero on Form 6251, line 43.

Note: ***Do not*** *decrease your section 1202 exclusion by the amount, if any, on line 12.*

Line 50

Generally, you may enter the amount, if any, from Schedule D, line 35, on Form 6251, line 50. However, if your qualified 5-year gain is different for the AMT (for example, because of a different basis), you must complete an AMT **Qualified 5-Year Gain Worksheet** (on page D-10 of the Schedule D instructions). If the amount on any line of the worksheet is different for the AMT, use the AMT amount instead of the regular tax amount. Enter the amount from line 8 of that worksheet on Form 6251, line 50.

Paperwork Reduction Act Notice. We ask for the information on this form to carry out the Internal Revenue laws of the United States. You are required to give us the information. We need it to ensure that you are complying with these laws and to allow us to figure and collect the right amount of tax.

You are not required to provide the information requested on a form that is subject to the Paperwork Reduction Act unless the form displays a valid OMB control number. Books or records relating to a form or its instructions must be retained as long as their contents may become material in the administration of any Internal Revenue law. Generally, tax returns and return information are confidential, as required by section 6103.

The time needed to complete and file this form will vary depending on individual circumstances. The estimated average time is: **Recordkeeping,** 19 min.; **Learning about the law or the form,** 1 hr., 14 min.; **Preparing the form,** 1 hr., 49 min.; **Copying, assembling, and sending the form to the IRS,** 34 min.

If you have comments concerning the accuracy of these time estimates or suggestions for making this form simpler, we would be happy to hear from you. See the instructions for the tax return with which this form is filed.

Form **6251**

Department of the Treasury
Internal Revenue Service (99)

Alternative Minimum Tax—Individuals

▶ See separate instructions.

▶ Attach to Form 1040 or Form 1040NR.

OMB No. 1545-0227

2003

Attachment Sequence No. **32**

Name(s) shown on Form 1040 | **Your social security number**

Part I Alternative Minimum Taxable Income (See instructions for how to complete each line.)

1	If filing Schedule A (Form 1040), enter the amount from Form 1040, line 38, and go to line 2. Otherwise, enter the amount from Form 1040, line 35, and go to line 7. (If zero or less, enter as a negative amount.)	1	
2	Medical and dental. Enter the **smaller** of Schedule A (Form 1040), line 4, **or** 2½% of Form 1040, line 35	2	
3	Taxes from Schedule A (Form 1040), line 9	3	
4	Certain interest on a home mortgage **not** used to buy, build, or improve your home	4	
5	Miscellaneous deductions from Schedule A (Form 1040), line 26	5	
6	If Form 1040, line 35, is over $139,500 (over $69,750 if married filing separately), enter the amount from line 9 of the worksheet for Schedule A (Form 1040), line 28	6	( )
7	Tax refund from Form 1040, line 10 or line 21	7	( )
8	Investment interest expense (difference between regular tax and AMT)	8	
9	Depletion (difference between regular tax and AMT)	9	
10	Net operating loss deduction from Form 1040, line 21. Enter as a positive amount	10	
11	Interest from specified private activity bonds exempt from the regular tax	11	
12	Qualified small business stock (see instructions)	12	
13	Exercise of incentive stock options (excess of AMT income over regular tax income)	13	
14	Estates and trusts (amount from Schedule K-1 (Form 1041), line 9)	14	
15	Electing large partnerships (amount from Schedule K-1 (Form 1065-B), box 6)	15	
16	Disposition of property (difference between AMT and regular tax gain or loss)	16	
17	Depreciation on assets placed in service after 1986 (difference between regular tax and AMT)	17	
18	Passive activities (difference between AMT and regular tax income or loss)	18	
19	Loss limitations (difference between AMT and regular tax income or loss)	19	
20	Circulation costs (difference between regular tax and AMT)	20	
21	Long-term contracts (difference between AMT and regular tax income)	21	
22	Mining costs (difference between regular tax and AMT)	22	
23	Research and experimental costs (difference between regular tax and AMT)	23	
24	Income from certain installment sales before January 1, 1987	24	( )
25	Intangible drilling costs preference	25	
26	Other adjustments, including income-based related adjustments	26	
27	Alternative tax net operating loss deduction	27	( )
28	**Alternative minimum taxable income.** Combine lines 1 through 27. (If married filing separately and line 28 is more than $191,000, see page 7 of the instructions.)	28	

Part II Alternative Minimum Tax

29 Exemption. (If this form is for a child under age 14, see page 7 of the instructions.)

IF your filing status is . . .	**AND line 28 is not over . . .**	**THEN enter on line 29 . . .**
Single or head of household	$112,500	$40,250
Married filing jointly or qualifying widow(er)	150,000	58,000
Married filing separately	75,000	29,000

If line 28 is **over** the amount shown above for your filing status, see page 7 of the instructions. — **29**

30	Subtract line 29 from line 28. If zero or less, enter -0- here and on lines 33 and 35 and stop here	30	
31	• If you reported capital gain distributions directly on Form 1040, line 13a; you reported qualified dividends on Form 1040, line 9b; **or** you had a gain on both lines 16 and 17a of Schedule D (Form 1040) (as refigured for the AMT, if necessary), complete Part III on the back and enter the amount from line 65 here. • **All others:** If line 30 is $175,000 or less ($87,500 or less if married filing separately), multiply line 30 by 26% (.26). Otherwise, multiply line 30 by 28% (.28) and subtract $3,500 ($1,750 if married filing separately) from the result.	31	
32	Alternative minimum tax foreign tax credit (see page 7 of the instructions)	32	
33	Tentative minimum tax. Subtract line 32 from line 31	33	
34	Tax from Form 1040, line 41 (minus any tax from Form 4972 and any foreign tax credit from Form 1040, line 44)	34	
35	**Alternative minimum tax.** Subtract line 34 from line 33. If zero or less, enter -0-. Enter here and on Form 1040, line 42	35	

For Paperwork Reduction Act Notice, see page 8 of the instructions. Cat. No. 13600G Form **6251** (2003)

Part III Tax Computation Using Maximum Capital Gains Rates

Caution: *If you **did not** complete Part IV of Schedule D (Form 1040), see page 8 of the instructions before you complete this part.*

Line	Description	Box	Amount
36	Enter the amount from Form 6251, line 30		36
37	Enter the amount from Schedule D (Form 1040), line 26, or line 13 of the Schedule D Tax Worksheet on page D-11 of the instructions for Schedule D (Form 1040), whichever applies (as refigured for the AMT, if necessary) (see page 8 of the instructions)	37	
38	Enter the amount from Schedule D (Form 1040), line 19 (as refigured for the AMT, if necessary) (see page 8 of the instructions)	38	
39	If you did not complete a Schedule D Tax Worksheet for the regular tax or the AMT, enter the amount from line 37. Otherwise, add lines 37 and 38, and enter the **smaller** of that result or the amount from line 10 of the Schedule D Tax Worksheet (as refigured for the AMT, if necessary)	39	
40	Enter the **smaller** of line 36 or line 39		40
41	Subtract line 40 from line 36		41
42	If line 41 is $175,000 or less ($87,500 or less if married filing separately), multiply line 41 by 26% (.26). Otherwise, multiply line 41 by 28% (.28) and subtract $3,500 ($1,750 if married filing separately) from the result ▶		42
43	Enter the amount from Schedule D (Form 1040), line 30, or line 19 of the Schedule D Tax Worksheet on page D-11 of the instructions for Schedule D (Form 1040), whichever applies (as figured for the regular tax) (see page 8 of the instructions)	43	
44	Enter the **smaller** of line 36 or line 37	44	
45	Enter the **smaller** of line 43 or line 44	45	
46	If you did not complete a Schedule D Tax Worksheet for the regular tax or the AMT, enter the amount from Schedule D (Form 1040), line 43 (or if that line is blank, the amount from Schedule D (Form 1040), line 31). Otherwise, enter the amount from line 32 of the Schedule D Tax Worksheet on page D-11 of the instructions for Schedule D (Form 1040) (or if that line is blank, the amount from line 20 of that worksheet). Refigure all amounts for the AMT, if necessary (see page 8 of the instructions)	46	
47	Enter the **smaller** of line 45 or line 46. If line 45 is zero, go to line 55	47	
48	Multiply line 47 by 5% (.05) ▶		48
49	Subtract line 47 from line 45. If zero or less, enter -0- and go to line 55	49	
50	Enter your qualified 5-year gain, if any, from Schedule D (Form 1040), line 35 (as refigured for the AMT, if necessary) (see page 8 of the instructions) — 50		
51	Enter the **smaller** of line 49 or line 50	51	
52	Multiply line 51 by 8% (.08) ▶		52
53	Subtract line 51 from line 49	53	
54	Multiply line 53 by 10% (.10) ▶		54
55	Subtract line 47 from line 46	55	
56	Subtract line 45 from line 44	56	
57	Enter the **smaller** of line 55 or line 56	57	
58	Multiply line 57 by 15% (.15) ▶		58
59	Subtract line 57 from line 56	59	
60	Multiply line 59 by 20% (.20) ▶		60
	If line 38 is zero or blank, skip lines 61 and 62 and go to line 63. Otherwise, go to line 61.		
61	Subtract line 44 from line 40	61	
62	Multiply line 61 by 25% (.25) ▶		62
63	Add lines 42, 48, 52, 54, 58, 60, and 62		63
64	If line 36 is $175,000 or less ($87,500 or less if married filing separately), multiply line 36 by 26% (.26). Otherwise, multiply line 36 by 28% (.28) and subtract $3,500 ($1,750 if married filing separately) from the result		64
65	Enter the **smaller** of line 63 or line 64 here and on line 31		65

appendix b: AMT Audits

All taxpayers are supposed to compute their taxes under the IRS tax table or schedules for the regular tax and the AMT. The greater of the two methods is what you pay.

If you do not do this, maybe thinking that the AMT cannot apply to you since your income is so low, you are likely to be audited. In an audit, the IRS will recompute your tax bill and mail you the Form 6251, a revised tax bill, and an explanation of why you owe the additional (AMT) tax, penalties, and interest.

This is known as a *correspondence audit*. This notice is computer-generated and it is possible that it is erroneous. Check it over carefully. If the IRS wants you to verify income, deductions, etc., *do so*. To ignore such a request is done at your financial peril. Moreover, this tax notice may require that you contact the IRS for a possible office audit.

If you do receive this notice, carefully read Publication 1, *Your Rights As A Taxpayer* and Publication 556, *Examination of Returns, Appeal Rights and Claims For*

Refund. These two publications are so important that they are included in this appendix.

The best way to get through an audit is to avoid being audited all together. Some points to remember to avoid an AMT audit in the first place include the following.

- Determine whether you owe an AMT, and if so, file Form 6251 and the MTC Form 8801.
- Be certain that all income items that are reported to the IRS by third parties (*e.g.*, your employer, bank, etc.) are reported on your Form 1040 and your Form 6251 that you file with the Form 1040.
- Keep all records for at least three years from filing your tax return (*e.g.*, 2004 return due on April 15, 2005—keep 2004 records at least until April 15, 2008) that may prove a tax deduction for AMT purposes.
- Keep all Forms 8801 to reflect your use of the AMT credit against future regular tax liability. This can result in an audit if your calculation disagrees with the IRS computer.
- If you legally shift expenses from Schedule A (itemized deductions) to Schedule C (profit or loss from business) to reduce the AMT bite, be prepared to prove to the IRS why you did so. Remember two very important points:
    1. taxpayers generally have the burden of proving their deductions and
    2. you can never take deductions in excess of your trade or business (Schedule C) income just to generate a tax loss.

- Do not assume that filing later than April 15th will not flag your return for audit. Remember, there is only an extension of time to file Form 1040 and Form 6251, *never* an extension to pay the tax owed, estimated, and due on April 15th. That includes the AMT.

In short, your AMT audit planning strategy should be to first avoid the audit and second, if not possible, to minimize the damage. Read the two IRS publications and respond to the IRS notices on a timely basis. Criminal penalties are usually not likely, unless the AMT was intentionally (fraudulently) evaded for several years. Lastly, and most importantly, retain the services of a qualified accountant or tax attorney to assist you in this process.

IRS

Department of the Treasury
Internal Revenue Service

Publication 1
(Rev. August 2000)

Catalog Number 64731W

www.irs.gov

Your Rights as a Taxpayer

The first part of this publication explains some of your most important rights as a taxpayer. The second part explains the examination, appeal, collection, and refund processes. This publication is also available in Spanish.

Declaration of Taxpayer Rights

I. Protection of Your Rights

IRS employees will explain and protect your rights as a taxpayer throughout your contact with us.

II. Privacy and Confidentiality

The IRS will not disclose to anyone the information you give us, except as authorized by law. You have the right to know why we are asking you for information, how we will use it, and what happens if you do not provide requested information.

III. Professional and Courteous Service

If you believe that an IRS employee has not treated you in a professional, fair, and courteous manner, you should tell that employee's supervisor. If the supervisor's response is not satisfactory, you should write to the IRS director for your area or the center where you file your return.

IV. Representation

You may either represent yourself or, with proper written authorization, have someone else represent you in your place. Your representative must be a person allowed to practice before the IRS, such as an attorney, certified public accountant, or enrolled agent. If you are in an interview and ask to consult such a person, then we must stop and reschedule the interview in most cases.

You can have someone accompany you at an interview. You may make sound recordings of any meetings with our examination, appeal, or collection personnel, provided you tell us in writing 10 days before the meeting.

V. Payment of Only the Correct Amount of Tax

You are responsible for paying only the correct amount of tax due under the law—no more, no less. If you cannot pay all of your tax when it is due, you may be able to make monthly installment payments.

VI. Help With Unresolved Tax Problems

The Taxpayer Advocate Service can help you if you have tried unsuccessfully to resolve a problem with the IRS. Your local Taxpayer Advocate can offer you special help if you have a significant hardship as a result of a tax problem. For more information, call toll free 1-877-777-4778 (1-800-829-4059 for TTY/TDD) or write to the Taxpayer Advocate at the IRS office that last contacted you.

VII. Appeals and Judicial Review

If you disagree with us about the amount of your tax liability or certain collection actions, you have the right to ask the Appeals Office to review your case. You may also ask a court to review your case.

VIII. Relief From Certain Penalties and Interest

The IRS will waive penalties when allowed by law if you can show you acted reasonably and in good faith or relied on the incorrect advice of an IRS employee. We will waive interest that is the result of certain errors or delays caused by an IRS employee.

THE IRS MISSION

PROVIDE AMERICA'S TAXPAYERS TOP QUALITY SERVICE BY HELPING THEM UNDERSTAND AND MEET THEIR TAX RESPONSIBILITIES AND BY APPLYING THE TAX LAW WITH INTEGRITY AND FAIRNESS TO ALL.

Examinations, Appeals, Collections, and Refunds

Examinations (Audits)

We accept most taxpayers' returns as filed. If we inquire about your return or select it for examination, it does not suggest that you are dishonest. The inquiry or examination may or may not result in more tax. We may close your case without change; or, you may receive a refund.

The process of selecting a return for examination usually begins in one of two ways. First, we use computer programs to identify returns that may have incorrect amounts. These programs may be based on information returns, such as Forms 1099 and W-2, on studies of past examinations, or on certain issues identified by compliance projects. Second, we use information from outside sources that indicates that a return may have incorrect amounts. These sources may include newspapers, public records, and individuals. If we determine that the information is accurate and reliable, we may use it to select a return for examination.

Publication 556, *Examination of Returns, Appeal Rights, and Claims for Refund,* explains the rules and procedures that we follow in examinations. The following sections give an overview of how we conduct examinations.

By Mail

We handle many examinations and inquiries by mail. We will send you a letter with either a request for more information or a reason why we believe a change to your return may be needed. You can respond by mail or you can request a personal interview with an examiner. If you mail us the requested information or provide an explanation, we may or may not agree with you, and we will explain the reasons for any changes. Please do not hesitate to write to us about anything you do not understand.

By Interview

If we notify you that we will conduct your examination through a personal interview, or you request such an interview, you have the right to ask that the examination take place at a reasonable time and place that is convenient for both you and the IRS. If our examiner proposes any changes to your return, he or she will explain the reasons for the changes. If you do not agree with these changes, you can meet with the examiner's supervisor.

Repeat Examinations

If we examined your return for the same items in either of the 2 previous years and proposed no change to your tax liability, please contact us as soon as possible so we can see if we should discontinue the examination.

Appeals

If you do not agree with the examiner's proposed changes, you can appeal them to the Appeals Office of IRS. Most differences can be settled without expensive and time-consuming court trials. Your appeal rights are explained in detail in both Publication 5, *Your Appeal Rights and How To Prepare a Protest If You Don't Agree,* and Publication 556, *Examination of Returns, Appeal Rights, and Claims for Refund.*

If you do not wish to use the Appeals Office or disagree with its findings, you may be able to take your case to the U.S. Tax Court, U.S. Court of Federal Claims, or the U.S. District Court where you live. If you take your case to court, the IRS will have the burden of proving certain facts if you kept adequate records to show your tax liability, cooperated with the IRS, and meet certain other conditions. If the court agrees with you on most issues in your case and finds that our position was largely unjustified, you may be able to recover some of your administrative and litigation costs. You will not be eligible to recover these costs unless you tried to resolve your case administratively, including going through the appeals system, and you gave us the information necessary to resolve the case.

Collections

Publication 594, *The IRS Collection Process,* explains your rights and responsibilities regarding payment of federal taxes. It describes:

- What to do when you owe taxes. It describes what to do if you get a tax bill and what to do if you think your bill is wrong. It also covers making installment payments, delaying collection action, and submitting an offer in compromise.
- IRS collection actions. It covers liens, releasing a lien, levies, releasing a levy, seizures and sales, and release of property.

Your collection appeal rights are explained in detail in Publication 1660, *Collection Appeal Rights.*

Innocent Spouse Relief

Generally, both you and your spouse are responsible, jointly and individually, for paying the full amount of any tax, interest, or penalties due on your joint return. However, if you qualify for innocent spouse relief, you may not have to pay the tax, interest, and penalties related to your spouse (or former spouse). For information on innocent spouse relief and two other ways to get relief, see Publication 971, *Innocent Spouse Relief,* and Form 8857, *Request for Innocent Spouse Relief (And Separation of Liability and Equitable Relief).*

Refunds

You may file a claim for refund if you think you paid too much tax. You must generally file the claim within 3 years from the date you filed your original return or 2 years from the date you paid the tax, whichever is later. The law generally provides for interest on your refund if it is not paid within 45 days of the date you filed your return or claim for refund. Publication 556, *Examination of Returns, Appeal Rights, and Claims for Refund,* has more information on refunds.

If you were due a refund but you did not file a return, you must file within 3 years from the date the return was originally due to get that refund.

Tax Information

The IRS provides a great deal of free information. The following are sources for forms, publications, and additional information.

- ***Tax Questions: 1-800-829-1040*** (1-800-829-4059 for TTY/TDD)
- ***Forms and Publications: 1-800-829-3676*** (1-800-829-4059 for TTY/TDD)
- ***Internet:*** **www.irs.gov**
- ***TaxFax Service:*** From your fax machine, dial ***703-368-9694.***
- ***Small Business Ombudsman:*** If you are a small business entity, you can participate in the regulatory process and comment on enforcement actions of IRS by calling **1-888-REG-FAIR.**
- ***Treasury Inspector General for Tax Administration:*** If you want to confidentially report misconduct, waste, fraud, or abuse by an IRS employee, you can call ***1-800-366-4484*** (1-800-877-8339 for TTY/TDD). You can remain anonymous.

Department of the Treasury
Internal Revenue Service

Publication 556
(Rev. August 2004)
Cat. No. 15104N

Examination of Returns, Appeal Rights, and Claims for Refund

Get forms and other information faster and easier by:

Internet • www.irs.gov or **FTP** • ftp.irs.gov

FAX • 703–368–9694 (from your fax machine)

Contents

Important Reminder 1
Introduction 1
Examination of Returns 2
Appeal Rights 8
Claims for Refund 12
How To Get Tax Help 15
Index 18

The IRS Mission

Provide America's taxpayers top quality service by helping them understand and meet their tax responsibilities and by applying the tax law with integrity and fairness to all.

Important Reminder

Fast track mediation. The IRS offers fast track mediation services to help taxpayers resolve many disputes resulting from:

- Examinations (audits),
- Offers in compromise,
- Trust fund recovery penalties, and
- Other collection actions.

See *Fast track mediation* under *If You Do Not Agree.*

Introduction

The Internal Revenue Service (IRS) accepts most federal tax returns as filed. However, the IRS examines (or audits) some returns to determine if income, expenses, and credits are being reported accurately.

If your return is selected for examination, it does not suggest that you made an error or are dishonest. Returns are chosen by computerized screening, by random sample, or by an income document matching program. See *Examination selection criteria*, later. You should also know that many examinations result in a refund or acceptance of the tax return without change.

This publication discusses general rules and procedures that the IRS follows in examinations. It explains what happens during an examination and your appeal rights, both within the IRS and in the federal court system. It also explains how to file a claim for refund of tax you already paid.

As a taxpayer, you have the right to be treated fairly, professionally, promptly, and courteously by IRS employees. Publication 1, Your Rights as a Taxpayer, explains your rights when dealing with the IRS.

Comments and suggestions. We welcome your comments about this publication and your suggestions for future editions.

You can email us at *taxforms@irs.gov*. Please put "Publications Comment" on the subject line.

You can write to us at the following address:

Internal Revenue Service
Individual Forms and Publications Branch
SE:W:CAR:MP:T:I
1111 Constitution Ave. NW
Washington, DC 20224

We respond to many letters by telephone. Therefore, it would be helpful if you would include your daytime phone number, including the area code, in your correspondence.

Useful Items

You may want to see:

Publication

- ❑ **1** Your Rights as a Taxpayer
- ❑ **5** Your Appeal Rights and How To Prepare a Protest If You Don't Agree
- ❑ **547** Casualties, Disasters, and Thefts
- ❑ **594** The IRS Collection Process
- ❑ **910** Guide to Free Tax Services
- ❑ **971** Innocent Spouse Relief (And Separation of Liability and Equitable Relief)
- ❑ **1546** The Taxpayer Advocate Service of the IRS
- ❑ **1660** Collection Appeal Rights
- ❑ **3605** Fast Track Mediation
- ❑ **3920** Tax Relief for Victims of Terrorist Attacks

Form (and Instructions)

- ❑ **843** Claim for Refund and Request for Abatement
- ❑ **1040X** Amended U.S. Individual Income Tax Return
- ❑ **2848** Power of Attorney and Declaration of Representative
- ❑ **4506** Request for Copy of Tax Return
- ❑ **4506-T** Request for Transcript of Tax Return
- ❑ **8379** Injured Spouse Claim and Allocation
- ❑ **8857** Request for Innocent Spouse Relief (And Separation of Liability and Equitable Relief)

See *How To Get Tax Help*, near the end of this publication, for information about getting these publications and forms.

Examination of Returns

Your return may be examined for a variety of reasons, and the examination may take place in any one of several ways. After the examination, if any changes to your tax are proposed, you can either agree with those changes and pay any additional tax you may owe, or you can disagree with the changes and appeal the decision.

Examination selection criteria. Your return may be selected for examination on the basis of computer scoring. A computer program called the Discriminant Inventory Function System (DIF) assigns a numeric score to each individual and some corporate tax returns after they have been processed. If your return is selected because of a high score under the DIF system, the potential is high that an examination of your return will result in a change to your income tax liability.

Your return may also be selected for examination on the basis of information received from third-party documentation, such as Forms 1099 and W-2, that does not match the information reported on your return. Or, your return may be selected to address both the questionable treatment of an item and to study the behavior of similar taxpayers (a market segment) in handling a tax issue.

In addition, your return may be selected as a result of information received from other sources on potential noncompliance with the tax laws or inaccurate filing. This information can come from a number of sources, including the media, public records, or informants. The information is evaluated for reliability and accuracy before it is used as the basis of an examination or investigation.

Notice of IRS contact of third parties. The IRS must give you reasonable notice before contacting other persons about your tax matters. You must be given notice that, in examining or collecting your tax liability, the IRS may contact third parties such as your neighbors, banks, employers, or employees. The IRS must also give you notice of specific contacts by providing you with a record of persons contacted on both a periodic basis and upon your request.

CAUTION *This provision does not apply:*

- *To any pending criminal investigation,*
- *When providing notice would jeopardize collection of any tax liability,*
- *Where providing notice may result in reprisal against any person, or*
- *When you authorized the contact.*

Taxpayer Advocate Service. The Taxpayer Advocate Service is an independent organization within the IRS whose goal is to help taxpayers resolve problems with the IRS. If you have an ongoing issue with the IRS that has not been resolved through normal processes, or you have suffered, or are about to suffer a significant hardship as a result of the administration of the tax laws, contact the Taxpayer Advocate Service.

TIP *Before contacting the Taxpayer Advocate, you should first discuss any problem with a supervisor. Your local Taxpayer Advocate will assist you if you are unable to resolve the problem with the supervisor.*

For more information, see Publication 1546. See *How To Get Tax Help*, near the end of this publication for more information about contacting the Taxpayer Advocate Service.

Comments on IRS enforcement actions. The Small Business and Agricultural Regulatory Enforcement Ombudsman and 10 Regional Fairness Boards have been established to receive comments from small business about federal agency enforcement actions. The Ombudsman will annually evaluate the enforcement activities of each agency and rate their responsiveness to small business. If you wish to comment on the enforcement actions of the IRS, you can take any of the following steps.

- Fax your comments to 1-202-481-5719.
- Write to the following address:
  Office of the National Ombudsman
  U.S. Small Business Administration
  409 3rd Street, SW
  Washington, DC 20416.
- Call 1-888-734-3247.
- Send an email to ombudsman@sba.gov.
- File a comment or complaint online at www.sba.gov.

If Your Return Is Examined

Some examinations are handled entirely by mail. Examinations not handled by mail can take place in your home, your place of business, an Internal Revenue office, or the office of your attorney, accountant, or enrolled agent. If the time, place, or method is not convenient for you, the examiner will try to work out something more suitable. However, the IRS makes the final determination of when, where, and how the examination will take place.

Throughout the examination, you can act on your own behalf or have someone represent you or accompany you. If you filed a joint return, either you or your spouse, or both, can meet with the IRS. You can have someone represent or accompany you. This person can be any federally authorized practitioner, including an attorney, a certified public accountant, an enrolled agent (a person enrolled to practice before the IRS), an enrolled actuary, or the person who prepared the return and signed it as the preparer.

If you want someone to represent you in your absence, you must furnish that person with proper written authorization. You can use Form 2848 or any other properly written authorization. If you want to consult with an attorney, a certified public accountant, an enrolled agent, or any other person permitted to represent a taxpayer during an interview for examining a tax return or collecting tax, you should make arrangements with that person to be available for the interview. In most cases, the IRS must suspend the interview and reschedule it. The IRS cannot suspend the interview if you are there because of an administrative summons.

Third party authorization. If you checked the box in the signature area of your income tax return (Form 1040, Form 1040A, or Form 1040EZ) to allow the IRS to discuss your return with another person (a third party designee), this authorization does not replace Form 2848. The box you checked on your return only authorizes the other person to receive information about the processing of your return and the status of your refund during the period your return is being processed. For more information, see the instructions for your return.

Confidentiality privilege. Generally, the same confidentiality protection that you have with an attorney also applies to certain communications that you have with federally authorized practitioners.

CAUTION *This confidentiality protection cannot be used by you in any administrative or court proceeding with an agency other than the IRS.*

Confidential communications are those that:

- Advise you on tax matters within the scope of the practitioner's authority to practice before the IRS,
- Would be confidential between an attorney and you, and
- Relate to noncriminal tax matters before the IRS, or
- Relate to noncriminal tax proceedings brought in federal court by or against the United States.

The confidentiality privilege does not apply to any written communication between a federally authorized practitioner and a corporate director, shareholder, officer, employee, agent, or representative in connection with the promotion of the corporation's participation in a tax shelter. A tax shelter is any entity, plan, or arrangement, a significant purpose of which is the avoidance or evasion of income tax.

Recordings. You can make an audio recording of the examination interview. Your request to record the interview should be made in writing. You must notify the examiner 10 days in advance and bring your own recording equipment. The IRS also can record an interview. If the IRS initiates the recording, you must be notified 10 days in advance and you can get a copy of the recording at your expense.

Transfers to another area. Generally, your return is examined in the area where you live. But if your return can be examined more quickly and conveniently in another area, such as where your books and records are located, you can ask to have the case transferred to that area.

Repeat examinations. The IRS tries to avoid repeat examinations of the same items, but sometimes this happens. If your tax return was examined for the same items in either of the 2 previous years and no change was proposed to your tax liability, please contact the IRS as soon as possible to see if the examination should be discontinued.

The Examination

An examination usually begins when you are notified that your return has been selected. The IRS will tell you which records you will need. The examination can proceed more easily if you gather your records before any interview.

Any proposed changes to your return will be explained to you or your authorized representative. It is important that you understand the reasons for any proposed changes. You should not hesitate to ask about anything that is unclear to you.

The IRS must follow the tax laws set forth by Congress in the Internal Revenue Code. The IRS also follows Treasury Regulations, other rules, and procedures that were written to administer the tax laws. The IRS also follows court decisions. However, the IRS can lose cases that involve taxpayers with the same issue and still apply its interpretation of the law to your situation.

Most taxpayers agree to changes proposed by examiners, and the examinations are closed at this level. If you do not agree, you can appeal any proposed change by following the procedures provided to you by the IRS. A more complete discussion of appeal rights is found later.

If You Agree

If you agree with the proposed changes, you can sign an agreement form and pay any additional tax you may owe. You must pay interest on any additional tax. If you pay when you sign the agreement, the interest is generally figured from the due date of your return to the date of your payment.

If you do not pay the additional tax when you sign the agreement, you will receive a bill that includes interest. If you pay the amount due within 10 business days of the billing date, you will not have to pay more interest or penalties. This period is extended to 21 calendar days if the amount due is less than $100,000.

If you are due a refund, you will receive it sooner if you sign the agreement form. You will be paid interest on the refund.

If the IRS accepts your tax return as filed, you will receive a letter in a few weeks stating that the examiner proposed no changes to your return. You should keep this letter with your tax records.

If You Do Not Agree

If you do not agree with the proposed changes, the examiner will explain your appeal rights. If your examination takes place in an IRS office, you can request an immediate meeting with the examiner's supervisor to explain your position. If an agreement is reached, your case will be closed.

If you cannot reach an agreement with the supervisor at this meeting, or if the examination took place outside of an IRS office, the examiner will write up your case explaining your position and the IRS' position. The examiner will forward your case for processing.

Fast track mediation. The IRS offers fast track mediation services to help taxpayers resolve many disputes resulting from:

- Examinations (audits),
- Offers in compromise,
- Trust fund recovery penalties, and
- Other collection actions.

Most cases that are not docketed in any court qualify for fast track mediation. Mediation can take place at a conference you request with a supervisor, or later. The process involves an Appeals Officer who has been trained in mediation. You may represent yourself at the mediation session, or someone else can act as your representative. For more information, see Publication 3605.

30-day letter and 90-day letter. Within a few weeks after your closing conference with the examiner and/or supervisor, you will receive a package with:

- A letter (known as a 30-day letter) notifying you of your right to appeal the proposed changes within 30 days,
- A copy of the examination report explaining the examiner's proposed changes,
- An agreement or waiver form, and
- A copy of Publication 5.

You generally have 30 days from the date of the 30-day letter to tell the IRS whether you will accept or appeal the proposed changes. The letter will explain what steps you should take, depending on which action you choose. Be sure to follow the instructions carefully. *Appeal Rights* are explained later.

90-day letter. If you do not respond to the 30-day letter, or if you later do not reach an agreement with an Appeals Officer, the IRS will send you a 90-day letter, which is also known as a notice of deficiency.

You will have 90 days (150 days if it is addressed to you outside the United States) from the date of this notice to file a petition with the Tax Court. Filing a petition with the Tax Court is discussed later under *Appeals to the Courts* and *Tax Court.*

TIP *The notice will show the 90th (and 150th) day by which you must file your petition with the Tax Court.*

Suspension of interest and penalties. Generally, the IRS has 3 years from the date you filed your return (or the date the return was due, if later) to assess any additional tax. However, interest and certain penalties will be suspended if the IRS does not mail a notice to you, stating your liability and the basis for that liability, within an 18-month period beginning on the later of:

- The date on which you timely filed your tax return, or
- The due date (without extensions) of your tax return.

If the IRS mails a notice stating your liability and the basis for that liability after the 18-month period, interest and certain penalties applicable to the suspension period will be suspended.

Note. For tax years beginning after 2003, the 18-month period is reduced to a 1-year period. Also, the suspension only applies if you filed your return by its due date (including extensions). The suspension does not apply for tax years ending before July 23,1998.

The suspension period begins the day after the close of the 18-month period (or 1-year) and ends 21 days after the IRS mails a notice to you stating your liability and the basis for that liability. Also, the suspension period applies separately to each notice stating your liability and the basis for that liability received by you.

CAUTION *The suspension does not apply to a:*

- *Failure-to-pay penalty,*
- *Fraudulent tax return,*
- *Penalty, interest, addition to tax, or additional amount with respect to any tax liability shown on your return, or*
- *Criminal penalty.*

If you later agree. If you agree with the examiner's changes after receiving the examination report or the 30-day letter, sign and return either the examination report or the waiver form. Keep a copy for your records. You can pay any additional amount you owe without waiting for a bill. Include interest on the additional tax at the applicable rate. This interest rate is usually for the period from the due date of the return to the date of payment. The examiner can tell you the interest rate(s) or help you figure the amount.

You must pay interest on penalties and on additional tax for failing to file returns, for overstating valuations, for understating valuations on estate and gift tax returns, and for substantially understating tax liability. Interest is generally figured from the date (including extensions) the tax return is required to be filed to the date you pay the penalty and/or additional tax.

If you pay the amount due within 10 business days after the date of notice and demand for immediate payment, you will not have to pay any additional penalties and interest. This period is extended to 21 calendar days if the amount due is less than $100,000.

How To Stop Interest From Accruing

If you think that you will owe additional tax at the end of the examination, you can stop the further accrual of interest by sending money to the IRS to cover all or part of the amount you think you will owe. Interest on part or all of any amount you owe will stop accruing on the date the IRS receives your money.

You can send an amount either in the form of a deposit in the nature of a cash bond or as a payment of tax. Both a deposit and a payment stop any further accrual of interest. However, making a deposit or payment will stop the accrual of interest on only the amount you sent. Because of compounding rules, interest will continue to accrue on accrued interest, even though you have paid the underlying tax.

TIP *To stop the accrual of interest on both tax and interest, you must make a deposit or payment for both the tax and interest that has accrued as of the date of deposit or payment.*

Payment or Deposit

Deposits differ from payments in two ways:

1. You can have all or part of your deposit returned to you without filing for a refund. However, if you request and receive your deposit and the IRS later assesses a deficiency for that period and type of tax, interest will be figured as if the funds were never on deposit. Also, your deposit will not be returned if one of the following situations applies:
   a. The IRS assesses a tax liability.
   b. The IRS determines, that by returning the deposit, it may not be able to collect a future deficiency.
   c. The IRS determines that the deposit should be applied against another tax liability.
2. Deposits do not earn interest. No interest will be included when a deposit is returned to you.

Notice not mailed. If you send money before the IRS mails you a notice of deficiency, you can ask the IRS to treat it as a deposit. You must make your request in writing.

If, after being notified of a proposed liability but before the IRS mails you a notice of deficiency, you send an amount large enough to cover the proposed liability, it will be considered a payment unless you request in writing that it be treated as a deposit.

If the amount you send is at least as much as the proposed liability and you do not request that it be treated as a deposit, the IRS will not send you a notice of deficiency. If you do not receive a notice of deficiency, you cannot take your case to the Tax Court. See *Tax Court,* later under *Appeal Rights.*

Notice mailed. If, after the IRS mails the notice of deficiency, you send money without written instructions, it will be treated as a payment. You will still be able to petition the Tax Court.

If you send money after receiving a notice of deficiency and you have specified in writing that it is a "deposit in the nature of a cash bond," the IRS will treat it as a deposit if you send it before either:

- The close of the 90-day or 150-day period for filing a petition with the Tax Court to appeal the deficiency, or
- The date the Tax Court decision is final, if you have filed a petition.

Using a Deposit To Pay the Tax

If you agree with the examiner's proposed changes after the examination, your deposit will be applied against any amount you may owe. The IRS will not mail you a notice of deficiency and you will not have the right to take your case to the Tax Court.

If you do not agree to the full amount of the deficiency after the examination, the IRS will mail you a notice of deficiency. Your deposit will be applied against the proposed deficiency unless you write to the IRS before the end of the 90-day or 150-day period stating that you still want the money to be treated as a deposit. You will still have the right to take your case to the Tax Court.

Installment Agreement Request

You can request a monthly installment plan if you cannot pay the full amount you owe. To be valid, your request must be approved by the IRS. However, if you owe $10,000 or less in tax and you meet certain other criteria, the IRS must accept your request.

TIP *Before you request an installment agreement, you should consider other less costly alternatives, such as a bank loan. You will continue to be charged interest and penalties on the amount you owe until it is paid in full. There is also a $43 fee if your installment agreement is approved.*

For more information about installment agreements, see Form 9465, Installment Agreement Request.

Interest Netting

If you owe interest to the IRS on an underpayment for the same period the IRS owes you interest on an overpayment, the IRS will figure interest on the underpayment and overpayment at the same interest rate (up to the amount of the overpayment). As a result, the net rate is zero for that period.

Abatement of Interest Due to Error or Delay by the IRS

The IRS may abate (reduce) the amount of interest you owe if the interest is due to an unreasonable error or delay by an IRS officer or employee performing a ministerial or managerial act (discussed later). Only the amount of interest on income, estate, gift, generation-skipping, and certain excise taxes can be reduced.

Note. Interest due to an error or delay in performing a managerial act can be reduced only if it accrued with respect to a deficiency or payment for a tax year beginning after July 30, 1996.

The amount of interest will not be reduced if you or anyone related to you contributed significantly to the error or delay. Also, the interest will be reduced only if the error or delay happened after the IRS contacted you in writing about the deficiency or payment on which the interest is based. An audit notification letter is such a contact.

The IRS cannot reduce the amount of interest due to a general administrative decision, such as a decision on how to organize the processing of tax returns.

Ministerial act. This is a procedural or mechanical act, not involving the exercise of judgment or discretion, during the processing of a case after all prerequisites (for example, conferences and review by supervisors) have taken place. A decision concerning the proper application of federal tax law (or other federal or state law) is not a ministerial act.

Example 1. You move from one state to another before the IRS selects your tax return for examination. A letter stating that your return has been selected is sent to your old address and then forwarded to your new address. When you get the letter, you respond with a request that the examination be transferred to the area office closest to your new address. The examination group manager approves your request. After your request has been approved, the transfer is a ministerial act. The IRS can reduce the interest because of any unreasonable delay in transferring the case.

Example 2. An examination of your return reveals tax due for which a notice of deficiency (90-day letter) will be issued. After you and the IRS discuss the issues, the notice is prepared and reviewed. After the review process, issuing the notice of deficiency is a ministerial act. If there is an unreasonable delay in sending the notice of deficiency to you, the IRS can reduce the interest resulting from the delay.

Managerial act. This is an administrative act during the processing of a case that involves the loss of records or the exercise of judgment or discretion concerning the management of personnel. A decision concerning the proper application of federal tax law (or other federal or state law) is not a managerial act.

Example. A revenue agent is examining your tax return. During the middle of the examination, the agent is sent to an extended training course. The agent's supervisor decides not to reassign your case, so the work is unreasonably delayed until the agent returns. Interest from the unreasonable delay can be abated since both the decision to send the agent to the training class and not to reassign the case are managerial acts.

How to request abatement of interest. You request an abatement (reduction) of interest on Form 843. You should file the claim with the IRS service center where you filed the tax return that was affected by the error or delay. If you do not remember the service center where you filed that tax return, send your claim to the service center where you filed your last tax return.

If you have already paid the interest and you would like a credit or refund of interest paid, you must file Form 843 within 3 years from the date you filed your original return or 2 years from the date you paid the interest, whichever is later. If you have not paid any of the interest, these time limitations for filing Form 843 do not apply.

Generally, you should file a separate Form 843 for each tax period and each type of tax. However, complete only one Form 843 if the interest is from an IRS error or delay that affected your tax for more than one tax period or for more than one type of tax (for example, where two or more tax years were being examined). You do not have to figure the dollar amounts of interest that you want lowered.

If your request for abatement of interest is denied, you can appeal the decision to the IRS Appeals Office.

Tax Court can review failure to abate interest. The Tax Court can review the IRS' refusal to abate (reduce) interest if all of the following requirements are met.

1. You filed a request for abatement of interest (Form 843) with the IRS after July 31,1996.
2. The IRS has mailed you a notice of final determination or a notice of disallowance.
3. You file a petition with the Tax Court within 180 days of the mailing of the notice of final determination or the notice of disallowance.

The following requirements must also be met.

1. For individual and estate taxpayers — your net worth must not exceed $2 million as of the filing date of your petition for review. For this purpose, individuals filing a joint return shall be treated as separate individuals.
2. For charities and certain cooperatives — you must not have more than 500 employees as of the filing date of your petition for review.
3. For all other taxpayers — your net worth must not exceed $7 million, and you must not have more than 500 employees as of the filing date of your petition for review.

Abatement of Interest for Individuals Affected by Presidentially Declared Disasters or Military or Terrorist Actions

If you are (or were) affected by a Presidentially declared disaster occurring after 1996 or a terrorist or military action occurring after September 10, 2001, the IRS may abate (reduce) the amount of interest you owe on certain taxes. The IRS may abate interest for the period of any additional time to file or pay that the IRS provides on account of the disaster or the terrorist or military action. The IRS will issue a notice or news release indicating who are affected taxpayers and stating the period of relief.

If you are eligible for relief from interest, but were charged interest for the period of relief, the IRS may retroactively abate your interest. To the extent possible, the IRS can take the following actions.

- Make appropriate adjustments to your account.
- Notify you when the adjustments are made.
- Refund any interest paid by you where appropriate.

For more information on disaster area losses, see *Disaster Area Losses* in Publication 547. For more information on other tax relief for victims of terrorist attacks, see Publication 3920.

Offer in Compromise

In certain circumstances, the IRS will allow you to pay less than the full amount you owe. If you think you may qualify, you should submit your offer by filing Form 656, Offer in Compromise. The IRS may accept your offer for any of the following reasons.

- There is doubt about the amount you owe (or whether you owe it).
- There is doubt as to whether you can pay the amount you owe based on your financial situation.
- An economic hardship would result if you had to pay the full amount owed.
- Your case presents compelling reasons that the IRS determines are a sufficient basis for compromise.

If your offer is rejected, you have 30 days to ask the Appeals Office of the IRS to reconsider your offer.

TIP *The IRS offers fast track mediation services to help taxpayers resolve many issues including a dispute regarding an offer in compromise. For more information, see Publication 3605.*

Generally, if you submit an offer in compromise, the IRS will delay certain collection activities. The IRS usually will not levy (take) your property to settle your tax bill during the following periods.

- While the IRS is evaluating your offer in compromise.

- The 30 days immediately after the offer is rejected.
- While your timely-filed appeal is being considered by Appeals.

Also, if the IRS rejects your original offer and you submit a revised offer within 30 days of the rejection, the IRS generally will not levy your property while it considers your revised offer.

For more information about submitting an offer in compromise, see Form 656.

Appeal Rights

Because people sometimes disagree on tax matters, the Service has an appeals system. Most differences can be settled within this system without expensive and time-consuming court trials.

However, your reasons for disagreeing must come within the scope of the tax laws. For example, you cannot appeal your case based only on moral, religious, political, constitutional, conscientious, or similar grounds.

In most instances, you may be eligible to take your case to court if you do not reach an agreement at your appeals conference, or if you do not want to appeal your case to the IRS Office of Appeals. See *Appeals to the Courts*, later, for more information.

Appeal Within the IRS

You can appeal an IRS tax decision to a local Appeals Office, which is separate from and independent of the IRS office taking the action you disagree with. The Appeals Office is the only level of appeal within the IRS. Conferences with Appeals Office personnel are held in an informal manner by correspondence, by telephone, or at a personal conference.

If you want an appeals conference, follow the instructions in the letter you received. Your request will be sent to the Appeals Office to arrange a conference at a convenient time and place. You or your representative should be prepared to discuss all disputed issues at the conference. Most differences are settled at this level.

If agreement is not reached at your appeals conference, you may be eligible to take your case to court. See *Appeals to the Courts*, later.

Protests and Small Case Requests

When you request an Appeals conference, you may also need to file either a formal written protest or a small case request with the office named in the letter you received. Also, see the special appeal request procedures in Publication 1660. In addition, for the appeal procedures for a spouse or former spouse of a taxpayer seeking relief from joint and several liability on a joint return, see Rev. Proc. 2003-19, which is on page 371 of the Internal Revenue Bulletin 2003-5 at www.irs.gov/pub/irs-irbs/irb03-05.pdf.

Written protest. You need to file a written protest in the following cases.

- All employee plan and exempt organization cases without regard to the dollar amount at issue.
- All partnership and S corporation cases without regard to the dollar amount at issue.
- All other cases, unless you qualify for the small case request procedure, or other special appeal procedures such as requesting Appeals consideration of liens, levies, seizures, or installment agreements.

If you must submit a written protest, see the instructions in Publication 5 about the information you need to provide. The IRS urges you to provide as much information as you can, as it will help speed up your appeal. That will save you both time and money.

CAUTION *Be sure to send the protest within the time limit specified in the letter you received.*

Small case request. If the total amount for any tax period is not more than $25,000, you may make a small case request instead of filing a formal written protest. In figuring the total amount, include a proposed increase or decrease in tax (including penalties), or claimed refund. If you are making an offer in compromise, include total unpaid tax, penalty, and interest due. For a small case request, follow the instructions in our letter to you by sending a letter:

- Requesting Appeals consideration,
- Indicating the changes you do not agree with, and
- Indicating the reasons why you do not agree.

Representation

You can represent yourself at your appeals conference, or you can be represented by any federally authorized practitioner, including an attorney, a certified public accountant, an enrolled actuary, or an enrolled agent.

If your representative attends a conference without you, he or she can receive or inspect confidential information only if you have filed a power of attorney or a tax information authorization. You can use a Form 2848 or any other properly written power of attorney or authorization.

You can also bring witnesses to support your position.

Confidentiality privilege. Generally, the same confidentiality protection that you have with an attorney also applies to certain communications that you have with federally authorized practitioners. See *Confidentiality privilege* under *If Your Return Is Examined*, earlier.

Appeals to the Courts

If you and the IRS still disagree after the appeals conference, you may be entitled to take your case to the United States Tax Court, the United States Court of Federal

Claims, or the United States District Court. These courts are independent of the IRS.

If you elect to bypass the IRS' appeals system, you may be able to take your case to one of the courts listed above. However, a case petitioned to the United States Tax Court will normally be considered for settlement by an Appeals Office before the Tax Court hears the case.

CAUTION *If you unreasonably fail to pursue the IRS' appeals system, or if your case is intended primarily to cause a delay, or your position is frivolous or groundless, the Tax Court may impose a penalty of up to $25,000. See* Appeal Within the IRS, *earlier.*

Prohibition on requests to taxpayers to give up rights to bring civil action. The Government cannot ask you to waive your right to sue the United States or a Government officer or employee for any action taken in connection with the tax laws. However, your right to sue can be waived if:

- You knowingly and voluntarily waive that right,
- The request to waive that right is made in writing to your attorney or other federally authorized practitioner, or
- The request is made in person and your attorney or other representative is present.

Burden of proof. For court proceedings resulting from examinations started after July 22, 1998, the IRS generally has the burden of proof for any factual issue if you have met the following requirements.

- You introduced credible evidence relating to the issue.
- You complied with all substantiation requirements of the Internal Revenue Code.
- You maintained all records required by the Internal Revenue Code.
- You cooperated with all reasonable requests by the IRS for information regarding the preparation and related tax treatment of any item reported on your tax return.
- You had a net worth of $7 million or less at the time your tax liability is contested in any court proceeding if your tax return is for a corporation, partnership, or trust.

CAUTION *The burden of proof does not change on an issue when another provision of the tax laws requires a specific burden of proof with respect to that issue.*

Use of statistical information. In the case of an individual, the IRS has the burden of proof in court proceedings based on any IRS reconstruction of income solely through the use of statistical information on unrelated taxpayers.

Penalties. The IRS has the burden of initially producing evidence in court proceedings with respect to the liability of any individual taxpayer for any penalty, addition to tax, or additional amount imposed by the tax laws.

Recovering litigation or administrative costs. These are the expenses that you pay to defend your position to the IRS or the courts. You may be able to recover reasonable litigation or administrative costs if all of the following conditions apply.

- You are the prevailing party.
- You exhaust all administrative remedies within the IRS.
- Your net worth is below a certain limit (see *Net worth requirements*, later).
- You do not unreasonably delay the proceeding.
- You apply for these costs within 90 days of the date on which the final decision of the IRS as to the determination of the tax, interest, or penalty was mailed to you.

Prevailing party, reasonable litigation costs, and reasonable administrative costs are explained later.

Note. If the IRS denies your award of administrative costs, and you want to appeal, you must petition the Tax Court within 90 days of the date on which the IRS mails the denial notice.

Prevailing party. Generally, you are the prevailing party if:

1. You substantially prevail with respect to the amount in controversy or on the most significant tax issue or set of issues in question, and
2. You meet the net worth requirements, discussed later.

You will not be treated as the prevailing party if the United States establishes that its position was substantially justified. The position of the United States is presumed not to be substantially justified if the IRS:

- Did not follow its applicable published guidance (such as regulations, revenue rulings, notices, announcements, and private letter rulings and determination letters issued to the taxpayer) in the proceeding (This presumption can be overcome by evidence.), or
- Has lost in courts of appeal for other circuits on substantially similar issues.

The court will generally decide who is the prevailing party.

Reasonable litigation costs. These include the following costs.

1. The reasonable costs of studies, analyses, engineering reports, tests, or projects found by the court to be necessary for the preparation of your case.
2. The reasonable costs of expert witnesses.

3. Attorney fees that generally may not exceed $150 per hour for calendar year 2004. The hourly rate is indexed for inflation. See *Attorney fees,* later.

Reasonable administrative costs. These include the following costs.

1. Any administrative fees or similar charges imposed by the IRS.
2. The reasonable costs of studies, analyses, engineering reports, tests, or projects.
3. The reasonable costs of expert witnesses.
4. Attorney fees that generally may not exceed $150 per hour for calendar year 2004. See *Attorney fees,* later.

Timing of costs. Administrative costs can be awarded for costs incurred after the earliest of:

- The date the first letter of proposed deficiency is sent that allows you an opportunity to request administrative review in the IRS Office of Appeals,
- The date you receive notice of the IRS Office of Appeals' decision, or
- The date of the notice of deficiency.

Net worth requirements. An individual taxpayer may be able to recover litigation or administrative costs if the following requirements are met.

- For individual and estate taxpayers — your net worth does not exceed $2 million as of the filing date of your petition for review. For this purpose, individuals filing a joint return are treated as separate individuals.
- For charities and certain cooperatives — you do not have more than 500 employees as of the filing date of your petition for review.
- For all other taxpayers — as of the filing date of your petition for review, your net worth does not exceed $7 million, and you must not have more than 500 employees.

Qualified offer rule. You can also receive reasonable costs and fees and be treated as a prevailing party in a civil action or proceeding if:

1. You make a qualified offer to the IRS to settle your case,
2. The IRS does not accept that offer, and
3. The tax liability (not including interest) later determined by the court is equal to or less than the amount of your qualified offer.

You must also meet the net worth requirements, discussed earlier, to get the benefit of the qualified offer rule.

Qualified offer. This is a written offer made by you during the qualified offer period. It must specify both the offered amount of your liability (not including interest) and that it is a qualified offer.

To be a qualified offer, it must remain open from the date it is made until the earliest of:

- The date it is rejected,
- The date the trial begins, or
- 90 days from the date it is made.

Qualified offer period. This period begins on the day the IRS mails you the first letter of proposed deficiency that allows you to request review by the IRS Office of Appeals. It ends 30 days before your case is first set for trial.

Attorney fees. For the calendar year 2004, the basic rate for attorney fees is $150 per hour and can be higher in certain circumstances. Those circumstances include the level of difficulty of the issues in the case and the local availability of tax expertise. The basic rate will be subject to a cost-of-living adjustment each year.

TIP *Attorney fees include the fees paid by a taxpayer for the services of anyone who is authorized to practice before the Tax Court or before the IRS. In addition, attorney fees can be awarded in civil actions for unauthorized inspection or disclosure of a taxpayer's return or return information.*

Fees can be awarded in excess of the actual amount charged if:

- You are represented for no fee, or for a nominal fee, as a pro bono service, and
- The award is paid to your representative or to your representative's employer.

Jurisdiction for determination of employment status. The Tax Court can review IRS employment status determinations (for example, whether individuals hired by you are in fact your employees or independent contractors) and the amount of employment tax under such determinations. Tax Court review can take place only if, in connection with an audit of any person, there is an actual controversy involving a determination by the IRS as part of an examination that either:

1. One or more individuals performing services for that person are employees of that person, or
2. That person is not entitled to relief under *Section 530(a) of the Revenue Act of 1978* (discussed later).

The following rules also apply to a Tax Court review of employment status.

- A Tax Court petition to review these determinations can be filed only by the person for whom the services are performed,
- If you receive a Notice of Determination by certified or registered mail, you must file a petition for Tax Court review must be filed within 90 days of the date of mailing of that notice (150 days if the notice is addressed to you outside the United States),

- If during the Tax Court proceeding, you begin to treat as an employee an individual whose employment status is at issue, the Tax Court will not consider that change in its decision,
- Assessment and collection of tax is suspended while the Tax Court review is taking place,
- There can be a *de novo* review by the Tax Court (a review which does not consider IRS administrative findings), and
- At your request and with the Tax Court's agreement, small tax case procedures (discussed later) are available to simplify the case resolution process when the amount at issue (including additions to tax and penalties) is $50,000 or less for each tax period involved.

For further information, see Publication 3953, Questions and Answers About Tax Court Proceedings for Determination of Employment Status Under IRC Section 7436.

Section 530(a) of the Revenue Act of 1978. This section relieves an employer of certain employment tax responsibilities for individuals not treated as employees. It also provides relief to taxpayers under audit or involved in administrative or judicial proceedings.

Tax Court review of request for relief from joint and several liability on a joint return. As discussed later, at *Relief from joint and several liability on a joint return* under *Claims for Refund*, you can request relief from liability for tax you owe, plus related penalties and interest, that you believe should be paid by your spouse (or former spouse). You also can petition (ask) the Tax Court to review your request for innocent spouse relief or separation of liability if either:

- The IRS sends you a determination notice denying, in whole or in part, your request, or
- You do not receive a determination notice from the IRS within 6 months from the date you file Form 8857.

If you receive a determination notice, you must petition the Tax Court to review your request during the 90-day period that begins on the date the IRS mails the notice. See Publication 971 for more information.

Note. Your spouse or former spouse may file a written protest and request an Appeals conference to protest your claim of innocent spouse relief or separation of liability.

Tax Court

You can take your case to the United States Tax Court if you disagree with the IRS over:

- Income tax,
- Estate tax,
- Gift tax, or
- Certain excise taxes of private foundations, public charities, qualified pension and other retirement plans, or real estate investment trusts.

For information on Tax Court review of a determination of employment status, see *Jurisdiction for determination of employment status*, earlier.

For information on Tax Court review of an IRS refusal to abate interest, see *Failure to abate interest may be reviewable by Tax Court*, earlier under *Examination of Returns*.

For information on Tax Court review of Appeals determinations with respect to lein notices and proposed levies, see Publication 1660.

You can take your case to the Tax Court before the IRS sends you a notice of deficiency. You can only appeal your case if you file a petition within 90 days from the date the notice is mailed to you (150 days if it is addressed to you outside the United States).

TIP *The notice will show the 90th (and 150th) day by which you must file your petition with the Tax Court.*

Note. If you consent, the IRS can withdraw a notice of deficiency. Once withdrawn, the limits on credits, refunds, and assessments concerning the notice are void, and you and the IRS have the rights and obligations that you had before the notice was issued. The suspension of any time limitation while the notice of deficiency was issued will not change when the notice is withdrawn.

CAUTION *After the notice is withdrawn, you cannot file a petition with the Tax Court based on the notice. Also, the IRS can later issue a notice of deficiency in a greater or lesser amount than the amount in the withdrawn deficiency.*

Generally, the Tax Court hears cases before any tax has been assessed and paid; however, you can pay the tax after the notice of deficiency has been issued and still petition the Tax Court for review. If you do not file your petition on time, the proposed tax will be assessed, a bill will be sent, and you will not be able to take your case to the Tax Court. Under the law, you must pay the tax within 21 days (10 business days if the amount is $100,000 or more). Collection can proceed even if you think that the amount is excessive. Publication 594 explains IRS collection procedures.

If you filed your petition on time, the court will schedule your case for trial at a location convenient to you. You can represent yourself before the Tax Court or you can be represented by anyone admitted to practice before that court.

Small tax case procedure. If the amount in your case is $50,000 or less for any one tax year or period, you can request that your case be handled under the small tax case procedure. If the Tax Court approves, you can present your case to the Tax Court for a decision that is final and that you cannot appeal. You can get more information regarding the small tax case procedure and other Tax Court matters from the United States Tax Court, 400 Second Street, N.W., Washington, DC 20217. More information can be found on the Tax Court's website at www.ustaxcourt.gov.

Motion to request redetermination of interest. In certain cases, you can file a motion asking the Tax Court to redetermine the amount of interest on either an underpayment or an overpayment. You can do this only in a situation that meets all of the following requirements.

1. The IRS has assessed a deficiency that was determined by the Tax Court.
2. The assessment included interest.
3. You have paid the entire amount of the deficiency plus the interest claimed by the IRS.
4. The Tax Court has found that you made an overpayment.

You must file the motion within one year after the decision of the Tax Court becomes final.

District Court and Court of Federal Claims

Generally, the District Court and the Court of Federal Claims hear tax cases only after you have paid the tax and filed a claim for a credit or refund. As explained later under *Claims for Refund,* you can file a claim with the IRS for a credit or refund if you think that the tax you paid is incorrect or excessive. If your claim is totally or partially disallowed by the IRS, you should receive a notice of claim disallowance. If the IRS does not act on your claim within 6 months from the date you filed it, you can then file suit for a refund.

You generally must file suit for a credit or refund no later than 2 years after the IRS informs you that your claim has been rejected. However, you can file suit if it has been 6 months since you filed your claim and the IRS has not yet delivered a decision.

You can file suit for a credit or refund in your United States District Court or in the United States Court of Federal Claims. However, you cannot appeal to the United States Court of Federal Claims if your claim is for credit or refund of a penalty that relates to promoting an abusive tax shelter or to aiding and abetting the understatement of tax liability on someone else's return.

For information about procedures for filing suit in either court, contact the Clerk of your District Court or of the United States Court of Federal Claims. For information on District Court review of Appeals determinations with respect to lien notices and proposed levies, see Publication 1660.

Refund or Credit of Overpayments Before Final Determination

Any court with proper jurisdiction, including the Tax Court, can order the IRS to refund any part of a tax deficiency that the IRS collects from you during a period when the IRS is not permitted to assess that deficiency, or to levy or engage in any court proceeding to collect that deficiency. In addition, the court can order a refund of any part of an overpayment determined by the Tax Court that is not at issue on appeal to a higher court. The court can order these refunds before its decision on the case is final.

Generally, the IRS is not permitted to take action on a tax deficiency during:

1. The 90-day (or 150-day if outside the United States) period that you have to petition a notice of deficiency to the Tax Court, or
2. The period that the case is under appeal if a bond is provided.

Claims for Refund

If you believe you have overpaid your tax, you have a limited amount of time in which to file a claim for a credit or refund. You can claim a credit or refund by filing Form 1040X. See *Time for Filing a Claim for Refund*, later.

File your claim by mailing it to the Internal Revenue service center where you filed your original return. File a separate form for each year or period involved. Include an explanation of each item of income, deduction, or credit on which you are basing your claim.

Corporations should file Form 1120X, Amended U.S. Corporation Income Tax Return, or other form appropriate to the type of credit or refund claimed.

TIP *See Publication 3920 for information on filing claims for tax forgiveness for individuals affected by terrorist attacks.*

Requesting a copy of your tax return. You can obtain a copy of the actual return and all attachments you filed with the IRS for an earlier year. This includes a copy of the Form W-2 or Form 1099 filed with your return. Use Form 4506 to make your request. You will be charged a fee, which you must pay when you submit Form 4506.

Requesting a copy of your tax account information. Use Form 4506-T, Request for Transcript of Tax Return, to request free copies of your tax return transcript, tax account transcript, record of account, verification of nonfiling, or Form W-2, Form 1099 series, Form 1098 series, or Form 5498 series transcript. The tax return transcript contains most of the line items of a tax return. A tax account transcript contains information on the financial status of the account, such as payments, penalty assessments, and adjustments. A record of account is a combination of line item information and later adjustments to the account. Form W-2, Form 1099 series, Form 1098 series, or Form 5498 series transcript contains data from these information returns.

Time for Filing a Claim for Refund

Generally, you must file a claim for a credit or refund within 3 years from the date you filed your original return or 2 years from the date you paid the tax, whichever is later. If you do not file a claim within this period, you may no longer be entitled to a credit or a refund.

If the due date to file a return or a claim for a credit or refund is a Saturday, Sunday, or legal holiday, it is filed on time if it is filed on the next business day. Returns you filed before the due date are considered filed on the due date. This is true even when the due date is a Saturday, Sunday, or legal holiday.

Disaster area claims for refund. If you live in a Presidentially declared disaster area or are affected by terroristic or military action, the deadline to file a claim for a refund may be postponed. This section discusses the special rules that apply to Presidentially declared disaster area refunds.

A Presidentially declared disaster is a disaster that occurred in an area declared by the President to be eligible for federal assistance under the Disaster Relief and Emergency Assistance Act.

Postponed refund deadlines. The IRS may postpone for up to 1 year the deadlines for filing a claim for refund. The postponement can be used by taxpayers who are affected by a presidentially declared disaster. The IRS may also postpone deadlines for filing income and employment tax returns, paying income and employment taxes, and making contributions to a traditional IRA or Roth IRA. For more information, see Publication 547.

If any deadline is postponed, the IRS will publicize the postponement in your area and publish a news release, revenue ruling, revenue procedure, notice, announcement, or other guidance in the Internal Revenue Bulletin.

TIP *A list of the areas eligible for assistance under the Disaster Relief and Emergency Assistance Act is available at the Federal Emergency Management Agency (FEMA) website at www.fema.gov and at the IRS website at www.irs.gov.*

Nonfilers can get refund of overpayments paid within 3-year period. The Tax Court can consider taxes paid during the 3-year period preceding the date of a notice of deficiency for determining any refund due to a nonfiler. This means that if you do not file your return, and you receive a notice of deficiency in the third year after the due date (with extensions) of your return and file suit with the Tax Court to contest the notice of deficiency, you may be able to receive a refund of excessive amounts paid within the 3-year period preceding the date of the notice of deficiency.

TIP *The IRS may postpone for up to 1 year certain tax deadlines, including the time for filing claims for refund, for taxpayers who are affected by a terrorist attack occurring after September 10, 2001. For more information, see Publication 3920.*

Claim for refund by estates electing the installment method of payment. In certain cases where an estate has elected to make tax payments through the installment method, the executor can file a suit for refund with a Federal District Court or the U.S. Court of Federal Claims before all the installment payments have been made. However, all the following must be true before a suit can be filed.

- The estate consists largely of an interest in a closely-held business.
- All installment payments due on or before the date the suit is filed have been made.
- No accelerated installment payments have been made.
- No Tax Court case is pending with respect to any estate tax liability.
- If a notice of deficiency was issued to the estate regarding its liability for estate tax, the time for petitioning the Tax Court has passed.
- No proceeding is pending for a declaratory judgment by the Tax Court on whether the estate is eligible to pay tax in installments.
- The executor has not included any previously litigated issues in the current suit for refund.
- The executor does not discontinue making installment payments timely, while the court considers the suit for refund.

TIP *If in its final decision on the suit for refund the court redetermines the estate's tax liability, the IRS must refund any part of the estate tax amount that is disallowed. This includes any part of the disallowed amount previously collected by the IRS.*

Limit on Amount of Refund

If you file your claim within 3 years after filing your return, the credit or refund cannot be more than the part of the tax paid within the 3 years (plus any extension of time for filing your return) before you filed the claim.

Example 1. You made estimated tax payments of $1,000 and got an automatic extension of time to August 15, 2000, to file your 1999 income tax return. When you filed your return on that date, you paid an additional $200 tax. Three years later, on August 15, 2003, you file an amended return and claim a refund of $700. Because you filed within the 3 years plus the 4-month extension period, you could get a refund of $700.

Example 2. The situation is the same as in Example 1, except that you filed your return on October 31, 2000, 2½ months after the extension period ended. You paid an additional $200 on that date. Three years later, on October 27, 2003, you file an amended return and claim a refund of $700. Although you filed your claim within 3 years from the date you filed your original return, the refund is limited to $200. The estimated tax of $1,000 was paid before the 3 years plus the 4-month extension period.

Claim filed after the 3-year period. If you file a claim after the 3-year period, but within 2 years from the time you paid the tax, the credit or refund cannot be more than the tax you paid within the 2 years immediately before you filed the claim.

Example. You filed your 1999 tax return on April 17, 2000. You paid $500 in tax. On November 2, 2001, after an examination of your 1999 return, you had to pay $200 in additional tax. On May 2, 2003, you file a claim for a refund of $300. Your refund will be limited to the $200 you paid during the 2 years immediately before you filed your claim.

Exceptions

The limits on your claim for refund can be affected by the type of item that forms the basis of your claim.

Special refunds. If you file a claim for refund based on one of the items listed below, the limits discussed earlier under *Time for Filing a Claim for Refund* may not apply. These special items are:

- A bad debt,
- A worthless security,
- A payment or accrual of foreign tax,
- A net operating loss carryback, and
- A carryback of certain tax credits.

The limits discussed earlier also may not apply if you have signed an agreement to extend the period of assessment of tax.

TIP *For information on special rules on filing claims for an individual affected by a terrorist attack, see Publication 3920.*

Periods of financial disability. If you are an individual (not a corporation or other taxpaying entity), the period of limitations on credits and refunds can be suspended during periods when you cannot manage your financial affairs because of physical or mental impairment that is medically determinable and either:

- Has lasted or can be expected to last continuously for at least 12 months, or
- Can be expected to result in death.

CAUTION *The period for filing a claim for refund will not be suspended for any time that someone else, such as your spouse or guardian, was authorized to act for you in financial matters.*

To claim financial disability, you generally must submit the following statements with your claim for credit or refund:

1. A written statement signed by a physician, qualified to make the determination, that sets forth:
   a. The name and a description of your physical or mental impairment,
   b. The physician's medical opinion that your physical or mental impairment prevented you from managing your financial affairs,
   c. The physician's medical opinion that your physical or mental impairment was or can be expected to result in death, or that it has lasted (or can be expected to last) for a continuous period of not less than 12 months, and
   d. To the best of the physician's knowledge, the specific time period during which you were prevented by such physical or mental impairment from managing your financial affairs, and
2. A written statement by the person signing the claim for credit or refund that no person, including your spouse, was authorized to act on your behalf in financial matters during the period described in paragraph (1)(d) of the physician's statement. Alternatively, if a person was authorized to act on your behalf in financial matters during any part of the period described in that paragraph, the beginning and ending dates of the period of time the person was so authorized.

CAUTION *The period of limitations will not be suspended on any claim for refund that (without regard to this provision) was barred as of July 22, 1998.*

Processing Claims for Refund

Claims are usually processed shortly after they are filed. Your claim may be denied, accepted as filed, or it may be examined. If a claim is examined, the procedures are almost the same as in the examination of a tax return.

However, if you are filing a claim for credit or refund based only on contested income tax or on estate tax or gift tax issues considered in previously examined returns and you do not want to appeal within the IRS, you should request in writing that the claim be immediately rejected. A notice of claim disallowance will then be promptly sent to you. You have 2 years from the date of mailing of the notice of disallowance to file a refund suit in the United States District Court or in the United States Court of Federal Claims.

Explanation of Any Claim for Refund Disallowance

The IRS must explain to you the specific reasons why your claim for refund is disallowed or partially disallowed. Claims for refund are disallowed based on a preliminary review or on further examination. Some of the reasons your claim may be disallowed include the following.

- It was filed late.
- It was based solely on the unconstitutionality of the revenue acts.
- It was waived as part of a settlement.
- It covered a tax year or issues which were part of a closing agreement or an offer in compromise.

- It was related to a return closed by a final court order.

If your claim is disallowed for these reasons, or any other reason, the IRS must send you an explanation.

Reduced Refund

Your refund may be reduced by an additional tax liability. Also, your refund may be reduced by amounts you owe for past-due child support, debts you owe to another federal agency, or past-due legally enforceable state income tax obligations. You will be notified if this happens. For those reductions, you cannot use the appeal and refund procedures discussed in this publication. However, you may be able to take action against the other agency.

Offset of past-due state income tax obligations against overpayments. Federal tax overpayments can be used to offset past-due, legally enforceable state income tax obligations. For the offset procedure to apply, your federal income tax return must show an address in the state that requests the offset. In addition, the state must first:

- Notify you by certified mail with return receipt that the state plans to ask for an offset against your federal income tax overpayment,
- Give you at least 60 days to show that some or all of the state income tax is not past due or not legally enforceable,
- Consider any evidence from you in determining that income tax is past due and legally enforceable,
- Satisfy any other requirements to ensure that there is a valid past-due, legally enforceable state income tax obligation, and
- Show that all reasonable efforts to obtain payment have been made before requesting the offset.

Past-due, legally enforceable state income tax obligation. This is an obligation (debt):

1. Established by a court decision or administrative hearing and no longer subject to judicial review, or
2. That is assessed, uncollected, can no longer be redetermined, and is less than 10 years overdue.

Offset priorities. Overpayments are offset in the following order.

1. Federal income tax owed.
2. Past-due child support.
3. Past-due, legally enforceable debt owed to a federal agency.
4. Past-due, legally enforceable state income tax debt.
5. Future federal income tax liability.

Note. If more than one state agency requests an offset for separate debts, the offsets apply against your overpayment in the order in which the debts accrued. In addition, state income tax includes any local income tax administered by the chief tax administration agency of a state.

Note. The Tax Court cannot decide the validity or merits of the credits or offsets (for example, collection of delinquent child support or student loan payments) made that reduce or eliminate a refund to which you were otherwise entitled.

Injured spouse exception. When a joint return is filed and only one spouse owes past-due child and spousal support or a federal debt, the other spouse can be considered an injured spouse. An injured spouse can get a refund for his or her share of the overpayment that would otherwise be used to pay the past-due amount.

To be considered an injured spouse, you must have:

1. Filed a joint return,
2. Received income (such as wages, interest, etc.),
3. Made tax payments (such as federal income tax withheld from wages or estimated tax payments) or claimed a refundable credit (such as the earned income credit), and
4. Reported the income and tax payments on the joint return.

If you are an injured spouse, you can obtain your portion of the joint refund by completing Form 8379. Follow the instructions on the form.

Relief from joint and several liability on a joint return. Generally, joint and several liability applies to all joint returns. This means that both you and your spouse (or former spouse) are liable for any tax shown on a joint return plus any understatement of tax that may become due later. This is true even if a divorce decree states that a former spouse will be responsible for any amounts due on previously filed joint returns.

In some cases, a spouse will be relieved of the tax, interest, and penalties on a joint tax return. Three types of relief are available.

- Innocent spouse relief.
- Separation of liability.
- Equitable relief.

Form 8857. Each kind of relief is different and has different requirements. You must file Form 8857 to request relief. See the instructions for Form 8857 and Publication 971 for more information on these kinds of relief and who may qualify for them.

How To Get Tax Help

You can get help with unresolved tax issues, order free publications and forms, ask tax questions, and get more information from the IRS in several ways. By selecting the method that is best for you, you will have quick and easy access to tax help.

Contacting your Taxpayer Advocate. If you have attempted to deal with an IRS problem unsuccessfully, you should contact your Taxpayer Advocate.

The Taxpayer Advocate independently represents your interests and concerns within the IRS by protecting your rights and resolving problems that have not been fixed through normal channels. While Taxpayer Advocates cannot change the tax law or make a technical tax decision, they can clear up problems that resulted from previous contacts and ensure that your case is given a complete and impartial review.

To contact your Taxpayer Advocate:

- Call the Taxpayer Advocate toll free at **1-877-777-4778.**
- Call, write, or fax the Taxpayer Advocate office in your area.
- Call **1-800-829-4059** if you are a TTY/TDD user.
- Visit the website at **www.irs.gov/advocate**.

For more information, see Publication 1546, *The Taxpayer Advocate Service of the IRS.*

Free tax services. To find out what services are available, get Publication 910, *Guide to Free Tax Services.* It contains a list of free tax publications and an index of tax topics. It also describes other free tax information services, including tax education and assistance programs and a list of TeleTax topics.

Internet. You can access the IRS website 24 hours a day, 7 days a week at **www.irs.gov** to:

- ***E-file.*** Access commercial tax preparation and *e-file* services available for free to eligible taxpayers.
- Check the amount of advance child tax credit payments you received in 2003.
- Check the status of your 2003 refund. Click on "Where's My Refund" and then on "Go Get My Refund Status." Be sure to wait at least 6 weeks from the date you filed your return (3 weeks if you filed electronically) and have your 2003 tax return available because you will need to know your filing status and the exact whole dollar amount of your refund.
- Download forms, instructions, and publications.
- Order IRS products on-line.
- See answers to frequently asked tax questions.
- Search publications on-line by topic or keyword.
- Figure your withholding allowances using our Form W-4 calculator.
- Send us comments or request help by email.
- Sign up to receive local and national tax news by email.
- Get information on starting and operating a small business.

You can also reach us using File Transfer Protocol at **ftp.irs.gov**.

Fax. You can get over 100 of the most requested forms and instructions 24 hours a day, 7 days a week, by fax. Just call **703-368-9694** from your fax machine. Follow the directions from the prompts. When you order forms, enter the catalog number for the form you need. The items you request will be faxed to you.

For help with transmission problems, call **703-487-4608.**

Long-distance charges may apply.

Phone. Many services are available by phone.

- *Ordering forms, instructions, and publications.* Call **1-800-829-3676** to order current-year forms, instructions, and publications and prior-year forms and instructions. You should receive your order within 10 days.
- *Asking tax questions.* Call the IRS with your tax questions at **1-800-829-1040.**
- *Solving problems.* You can get face-to-face help solving tax problems every business day in IRS Taxpayer Assistance Centers. An employee can explain IRS letters, request adjustments to your account, or help you set up a payment plan. Call your local Taxpayer Assistance Center for an appointment. To find the number, go to **www.irs.gov** or look in the phone book under "United States Government, Internal Revenue Service."
- *TTY/TDD equipment.* If you have access to TTY/TDD equipment, call **1-800-829-4059** to ask tax or account questions or to order forms and publications.
- *TeleTax topics.* Call **1-800-829-4477** to listen to pre-recorded messages covering various tax topics.
- *Refund information.* If you would like to check the status of your 2003 refund, call **1-800-829-4477** for automated refund information and follow the recorded instructions or call **1-800-829-1954**. Be sure to wait at least 6 weeks from the date you filed your return (3 weeks if you filed electronically) and have your 2003 tax return available because you will need to know your filing status and the exact whole dollar amount of your refund.

Evaluating the quality of our telephone services. To ensure that IRS representatives give accurate, courteous, and professional answers, we use several methods to evaluate the quality of our telephone services. One method is for a second IRS representative to sometimes listen in on or record telephone calls. Another is to ask some callers to complete a short survey at the end of the call.

Walk-in. Many products and services are available on a walk-in basis.

- *Products.* You can walk in to many post offices, libraries, and IRS offices to pick up certain forms, instructions, and publications. Some IRS offices, libraries, grocery stores, copy centers, city and county government offices, credit unions, and office supply stores have a collection of products available to print from a CD-ROM or photocopy from reproducible proofs. Also, some IRS offices and libraries have the Internal Revenue Code, regulations, Internal Revenue Bulletins, and Cumulative Bulletins available for research purposes.
- *Services.* You can walk in to your local Taxpayer Assistance Center every business day to ask tax questions or get help with a tax problem. An employee can explain IRS letters, request adjustments to your account, or help you set up a payment plan. You can set up an appointment by calling your local Center and, at the prompt, leaving a message requesting Everyday Tax Solutions help. A representative will call you back within 2 business days to schedule an in-person appointment at your convenience. To find the number, go to **www.irs.gov** or look in the phone book under "United States Government, Internal Revenue Service."

Mail. You can send your order for forms, instructions, and publications to the Distribution Center nearest to you and receive a response within 10 workdays after your request is received. Use the address that applies to your part of the country.

- **Western part of U.S.:**
  Western Area Distribution Center
  Rancho Cordova, CA 95743–0001
- **Central part of U.S.:**
  Central Area Distribution Center
  P.O. Box 8903
  Bloomington, IL 61702–8903
- **Eastern part of U.S. and foreign addresses:**
  Eastern Area Distribution Center
  P.O. Box 85074
  Richmond, VA 23261–5074

CD-ROM for tax products. You can order IRS Publication 1796, *Federal Tax Products on CD-ROM,* and obtain:

- Current-year forms, instructions, and publications.
- Prior-year forms and instructions.
- Frequently requested tax forms that may be filled in electronically, printed out for submission, and saved for recordkeeping.
- Internal Revenue Bulletins.

Buy the CD-ROM from National Technical Information Service (NTIS) on the Internet at **www.irs.gov/cdorders** for $22 (no handling fee) or call **1–877–233–6767** toll free to buy the CD-ROM for $22 (plus a $5 handling fee). The first release is available in early January and the final release is available in late February.

CD-ROM for small businesses. IRS Publication 3207, *Small Business Resource Guide,* is a must for every small business owner or any taxpayer about to start a business. This handy, interactive CD contains all the business tax forms, instructions and publications needed to successfully manage a business. In addition, the CD provides an abundance of other helpful information, such as how to prepare a business plan, finding financing for your business, and much more. The design of the CD makes finding information easy and quick and incorporates file formats and browsers that can be run on virtually any desktop or laptop computer.

It is available in early April. You can get a free copy by calling **1–800–829–3676** or by visiting the website at **www.irs.gov/smallbiz**.

Index

A

accelerated depreciation (pre-1987), 63, 64, 131
accelerating income, 104, 113
accounts receivable, 108
Action on Decision, 100
add back, 12, 25, 26, 27, 29, 31, 32, 33, 35, 36, 37, 40, 44
adjusted gross income (AGI), 32–35, 41–45, 122, 123, 132, 136, 138, 140
adjustments, 5, 8, 21, 22, 23, 24, 28, 33, 42, 45–57, 61, 63, 64, 72, 88, 89, 90, 92, 105, 115, 116, 117, 124, 126, 127, 132–135, 137, 139, 141, 143, 144
adoption credits, 80
AGI floor, 33, 34, 35, 44, 122, 123
alcohol fuel credit, 48
alternative depreciation system (ADS), 51
alternative minimum taxable income (AMTI), 8, 11, 12, 14, 22, 25, 26, 27, 29, 31, 35, 36, 37, 40, 42, 45, 46, 47, 49, 50, 51, 52, 53, 54, 55, 57, 61, 63, 64, 65, 69, 71, 87, 105, 109, 116, 118, 126, 134, 135, 137, 139, 141
alternative tax NOL deduction (ATNOLD), 54
American Jobs Creation Act of 2004, 36, 87, 123
AMT basis, 124, 125
AMT planning strategies, 103, 111
AMT rates, 13, 14, 107, 113
AMT roadmap, 8
AMT worksheet, 6
AMT-ADS, 51, 52
AMT-NOL, 54
AMT-PAL, 55
AMT-TPI, 68
AMTFTC, 9, 80, 88
  limitation, 87
annuities, 28, 34
appraisal fees, 33
Audit Guides, 102
audits, 98

B

bankruptcy, 22
basis adjustment, 48, 49

C

capital assets, 107, 108, 111
capital gains, 17, 28, 49, 68, 104, 107–112, 117, 118, 136
casualty and theft losses, 34, 49
charitable contributions, 42, 113, 131
Chief Counsel Advice Memoranda, 102
child tax credit, 80
circulation costs, 48, 50, 89
credit for the elderly and permanently and totally disabled, 80
credits, 67, 79, 92, 107, 129
crossover point, 104, 105
Cumulative Bulletin, 99

D

DC homebuyer credit, 80
dealer held commodity derivative financial investments, 108
deductions, 1, 67, 104
deferral items, 88, 90
Department of Commerce, 37
dependency exemptions. *See personal exemptions*
dependent care credit, 80
depletion, 63, 65, 90
depreciable real estate, 108
depreciation, 33, 48, 49, 51, 56, 57, 63, 64, 65, 88, 89, 90, 99, 124, 131, 134, 135

E

early retirement, 21
education expenses, 31
elective deferrals and IRA contributions credit, 80
employee groups, 35
employment agency fees, 34
exclusion preferences, 127
exclusions, 67, 103
executives, 21
exemptions, 5, 8, 11, 17, 24–27, 40–44, 64, 67, 95, 103, 106, 112, 131, 133, 134, 136, 137, 141
expenses, 113, 125
extractive industries, 65

F

farming syndicates, 61
fees to collect income, 33
Field Service Advice Memoranda, 103
foreign tax credit, 79, 80, 81, 87, 107
  limitation, 86, 87
foreign taxes, 36, 86, 87, 131
Form 1040, 2, 5, 6, 9, 13, 17, 22, 40, 41, 44, 45, 46, 54, 68, 71, 74, 111, 119, 131, 136, 138, 140
Form 1040 NR, 81, 86
Form 1065, 55
Form 1099, 126
Form 1116, 80
Form 4684, 49
Form 4797, 49
Form 4835, 56
Form 4952, 74
Form 6251, 2, 5, 6, 9, 11, 12, 13, 17, 22, 24, 28, 40, 41, 44, 46, 48, 54, 55, 56, 61, 63, 66, 69, 72, 74, 119, 133, 135, 137, 139, 141, 142
Form 8582, 56
Form 8801, 91

G

gambling losses, 34
general business credit, 49
General Counsel Memorandum, 100
generation skipping transfer tax, 125

H

head of household, 5
health savings accounts (HSAs), 32

hedging transactions, 108
hobby expenses, 33
home mortgage interest, 23, 24, 31, 72, 104, 120, 121, 126, 129, 131, 132
Hope and Lifetime Learning credits, 80

I

impairment related work expenses, 34
incentive plans, 22
incentive stock options, 21, 22, 89, 117, 118, 119, 127, 129
income in respect of a decedent, 34
income-producing property, 34
inflation, 13, 118
installment sales, 48, 52, 89
intangible drilling costs, 63, 65, 66, 89
intangible property, 108
intellectual property, 108
Internal Revenue Code, 97
Internal Revenue Manual, 102
Internal Revenue Service (IRS), 1, 2, 5, 11, 13, 32, 35, 41, 45, 96, 97, 98, 99, 100, 101, 102, 103, 106, 110, 152
inventory, 108
investment fees, 33
investment interest expense, 72
investments, 28
itemized deductions, 25, 26, 27, 28, 33, 34, 36, 40, 41, 42, 44, 45, 90, 113, 114, 124, 125, 132, 133, 136, 138, 141
itemized elected, 45

J

job search fees, 34

K

Klaassen v. Commissioner, 43

L

legal expenses, 33
license fees, 34
limitation on deductions, 21, 23, 28
long-term capital gains, 17, 109, 111, 112, 129, 130
long-term contracts, 48, 53, 89
loss limitations, 89
loss on deposits, 33

M

MACRS. *See modified accelerated cost recovery system*
married filing joint, 5, 11, 13, 14, 25, 26, 103, 131
married filing separately, 11, 12, 14, 103
medical expenses, 23, 27, 32, 33, 42, 122, 126, 129, 131, 132, 134, 140
middle-class taxpayers, 1, 48
minimum tax credit (MTC), 79, 88–92, 105, 106, 115, 116, 127, 128, 135
mining costs, 48, 54, 89

minors, 12
miscellaneous deductions, 23, 27, 33, 34, 35, 44, 90, 113, 114, 123, 126, 129, 133, 134
modified accelerated cost recovery system (MACRS), 51, 57, 65
mortgage credit, 80
mortgages. *See home mortgage interest*
municipal bonds (MUNI), 69, 70, 71, 76
mutual funds, 17

N

net operating loss (NOL), 48, 54
nonitemized deductions, 24, 29, 40, 124
nonrefundable personal credits, 79, 80

O

oil and gas partnerships, 65
ordinary income, 107, 109, 111, 112, 118

P

passive activity losses, 48, 55, 56, 61, 90, 104
percentage depletion, 65
percentage-of-completion method, 53
personal exemptions, 24, 40, 44, 64, 129, 131, 133, 134, 136, 137, 141
phaseout, 11, 17
physical or mental disability expenses, 34
pollution control facilities, 48, 56
premiums on taxable bonds, 34
private activity bond (PAB), 69–76, 126, 127, 130
Private Letter Ruling, 101
professional society dues, 34
property dispositions, 89
property taxes, 24, 25, 26, 27, 36, 37, 39, 104, 112, 131, 134, 140
Publication 17, 35, 106
Publication 514, 80

Q

qualified bonds, 70
qualified housing interest. *See home mortgage interest*
qualifying travel and transportation costs, 34

R

raw land, 108
refunds, 1
regular tax, 1, 2, 6, 9, 12, 13, 14, 17, 22, 23, 25–28, 31–36, 41, 43, 44, 45, 48–57, 61, 65, 66, 68–76, 79, 80, 81, 86–90, 105, 106, 110–127, 131, 133–141
rental property, 108
research and development costs, 90
Restructuring and Reform Act of 1998, 2

résumé costs, 34
return-free tax system, 2
Revenue Procedures, 99
Revenue Rulings, 99

S

safe deposit box rental, 33, 131
sales taxes, 36, 112
Sarbanes-Oxley Act, 119
saver's credit, 80
Schedule A, 29, 35, 36, 41, 42, 113, 114
Schedule C, 45, 46, 54, 56, 106, 113, 114, 123
Schedule D, 17, 49, 68, 136
Schedule K-1, 55
Section 83(b) tax election, 118
self-employment tax, 125
single filers, 5, 11, 14, 27, 28, 40, 49, 52, 103, 104, 114, 120, 138, 139
small business stock exclusion, 63, 66, 68, 90
standard deduction, 24, 26, 40, 44, 45, 64, 125, 126, 129, 136, 137, 140, 141
state taxes, 23, 24, 36, 37, 40, 42, 45, 46, 69, 112, 129, 131, 134, 138
stock appreciation rights (SARS), 119
stock options, 22
straight line depreciation, 64
supplies, 108
surviving spouse, 5, 11, 14

T

tangible personal property, 108
tax planning, 95, 96, 97
tax preference items, 5, 8, 42, 63–72, 73, 76, 77, 90, 92, 97, 105, 116, 126, 134, 135
tax preparation fees, 33
Tax Reform Act, 55, 70, 71
tax shelter farm activity, 48, 61
tax-exempt interest, 63, 69, 90, 129
taxable income, 5, 8, 111
Taxpayer Relief Act of 1997, 51
Technical Advice Memorandum, 102
tools used in job, 34
total tax liability, 25, 26, 28, 43, 114, 115, 116, 118, 142
Treasury Regulations, 98
trust fees, 33

U

U.S. Treasury, 2
uniforms, 34
unreimbursed employee expenses, 34

W

work clothes, 34
Working Families Tax Relief Act, 80

About the Author

Harold Peckron is a nationally recognized expert on the Alternative Minimum Tax, with a tax career that spans more than three decades. In addition to writing on the subject, he has taught tax as a tenured law professor and as a seminar leader to professional groups. He has served in government and private industry.

During this career, he has had the opportunity to work with individuals, not-for-profit and for-profit companies, and foreign entities. He has written over four dozen tax articles and a dozen books on tax, including specialized tax subjects of pricing a company and revenue recognition.

Some of the most fulfilling aspects of his career have involved community and business volunteer work that aided struggling and first-time entrepreneurs. Over the years he has participated in Junior Achievement lectures in business to youth and served in the Volunteer Income Assistance program for low income and elderly taxpayers.

Mr. Peckron holds several graduate degrees, including an LL.M. in Taxation from the Georgetown University Law School. His interests include running marathons and writing. He lives in Florida.